The A to Z *of* Wedding Worries

... and how to put them right

Suzan St Maur

Published by How To Books Ltd
Spring Hill House
Spring Hill Road
Begbroke, Oxford OX5 1RX
Tel: (01865) 375794. Fax: (01865) 379162
email: info@howtobooks.co.uk
www.howtobooks.co.uk

British Library Cataloguing in Publication Data
A catalogue record for this book is available from the British
Library

ISBN 978 1 84528 172 4

Cartoons by Phillip Burrows
Produced for How to Books by Deer Park Productions, Tavistock
Typeset by Pantek Arts Ltd, Maidstone, Kent
Printed and bound by Bell & Bain Ltd, Glasgow

NOTE: The material contained in this book is set out in good
faith for general guidance and no liability can be accepted
for loss or expense incurred as a result of relying in particular
circumstances on statements made in this book. Laws and
regulations are complex and liable to change, and readers should
check the current position with the relevant authorities before
making personal arrangements.

A ^{The} to Z

$_{of}$
Wedding Worries

howtobooks

Please send for a free copy of the latest catalogue to:
How To Books
Spring Hill House, Spring Hill Road,
Begbroke, Oxford OX5 1RX, United Kingdom
e-mail: info@howtobooks.co.uk
http://www.howtobooks.co.uk

Contents

About the author

Canadian-born Suzan St Maur is a researcher, writer and author specialising in business, consumer and humour topics. She has extensive experience of writing across all media in both corporate and entertainment fields, and is also well known as a business and humorous columnist on hundreds of websites internationally. As well as writing her own material she edits other people's books, scripts and text, and advises on book preparation and publication.

She has written 16 published books including the popular *Wedding Speeches For Women*, also by How To Books.

Suzan lives in Bedfordshire, UK, with her teenage son and various pets. She has been married more than once and consequently has personal experience of most of the main issues affecting weddings!

You can read more about Suzan and her work on her website – www.suzanstmaur.com

Other books by Suzan St Maur

- *The Jewellery Book* (*with Norbert Streep*) (Magnum)

- *The Home Safety Book* (Jill Norman Books)

- *The A to Z of Video and AV Jargon* (Routledge)

- *Writing Words That Sell* (*with John Butman*) (Management Books 2000)

- *Writing Your Own Scripts and Speeches* (McGraw-Hill)

- *The Horse Lover's Joke Book* (Kenilworth Press)

- *Powerwriting* (Prentice Hall Business)

- *Canine Capers* (Kenilworth Press)

- *The Food Lover's Joke Book* (ItsCooking.com)

- *Get Yourself Published* (LeanMarketing Press)

- *The MAMBA Way to Make Your Words Sell* (LeanMarketing Press)

- *The Easy Way to Be Brilliant at Business Writing* (LeanMarketing Press)

- *Wedding Speeches for Women* (How To Books)

- *The Country-Lover's Joke Book* (Merlin Unwin Books)

Acknowledgements

My heartfelt thanks go to the many people from all over the world who contributed their expertise and experiences to this book, including:

Anya

Barbara Grengs

Bernadette Chapman

Britt Armstrong Gash

Christine

David Long

Dom Pannell

Faye Cassidy

Geoff Beattie

'Ishrugged'

Jonathan Heywood

Julie

Karen

Kay Mussellwhite

Kelly Chandler

'Kikonie'

Lesley Chapman

Lori Osterberg

Lynn

Namrata Manot

Nick and Sandra

Nick Terry

Nikki Read

Peter Jones

Peter Snell

Sally Farmiloe-Neville

'Screenmom'

(Dr) Simon Raybould

Steve Wilson

Sue Malleson

Sue McGaughran

Susan Macaulay

Steve Haley

Tammie Scott

Tom Crellin

Tom Webb

Warren Cass

Yakir Zur

Dedication

To all the girls on BB – with my love and thanks for being such good friends.

Introduction

Wedding worries ...

Now who would want to write a book like this? Surely all weddings are fairytales made in some Nirvana-like place and can't possibly present any problems?

Uh-uh. You know, and I know, that this just isn't true.

Funnily enough the inspiration for this book came from someone who read my last one, *Wedding Speeches for Women*, and emailed How To Books asking how they should handle things if the bride's parents were divorced.

How To Books and I had a chat and realised that there are many more potentially tricky issues in the planning and implementing of a wedding that can worry the you-know-what out of everyone. Yet most of the time these issues can be resolved, provided that you're aware of them and have some solutions up your sleeve.

That's why this book is here now – helping not only to solve any problems, but in many cases also to anticipate them – and deal with them – before they get the chance to become a problem.

A source of comfort when you're worried or troubled by something connected with your wedding.

A source of reassurance where your concerns are probably unfounded, but worry you just the same.

Where there are questions, here are some answers.

Give me a shout if you need to share a wedding-related problem, here ... suze@suzanstmaur.com. I can't guarantee I'll solve every problem, but I will certainly try to refer you to some information that may help.

By the way... a quick word about the nuts and bolts element of this book.

If you see this sort of type, **this is an example**, when I suggest you key the information into Google or another search engine, please make sure you use all the characters – including the inverted commas/quotation marks if shown. That way you'll get a better result from your search.

And now (with the help of this book) ... relax, smile, enjoy, and have a wonderful, wonderful wedding day.

SUZE
suze@suzanstmaur.com

Alcohol

How much for the bridal party?

Many people believe that a couple of drinks loosen the tongue, relax inhibitions, decrease stress and allow you to perform better.

Whereas all that may be true, alcohol also makes you drunk.

Of course you may want to have a nip of brandy or a glass of champagne before you set out for your wedding, but whatever you do, don't have any more than one or two units. It's amazing how little alcohol it takes to affect your co-ordination and that's a problem you really don't need if you're navigating your way up stone steps in an unfamiliarly long dress with a train behind you and a veil in front of your face.

Equally, bear in mind that during the ceremony and at the reception the whole bridal party needs to be able to concentrate on what is going on. A drunken best man can be a nightmare, especially when he gets up to speak. (Also see section titled Speeches.)

A

Realistically there's not a lot you can do to prevent people from over-drinking if they are absolutely insistent on doing so, but certainly you can make it crystal clear to everyone that you want them to stay sober until after the speeches.

Drunkenness at receptions is the source of many a funny story as well as an equal number of disaster tales. If you want to avoid the latter, ask a few reliable family members or friends to keep an eye open for anyone who is getting overly refreshed. That person should then be keenly encouraged to drink plenty of water or soft drinks and should be escorted out into the fresh air for a while – and if push comes to shove, escorted into a taxi home.

Drunken fights can occur quite easily at weddings, with booze exacerbating any existing tensions between individuals and reducing inhibitions at the same time. Once again, it pays to ask those reliable family members or friends to be on the watch for any 'trouble' and to nip it in the bud should it start. You're likely to know beforehand who among the guests are candidates for a disagreement; try to keep them well away from each other and warn others to be wary.

Drunk at reception

I lived with a mobile DJ for three years and went to most of his gigs with him. We worked a lesbian wedding once. It all went very well, and was extremely tasteful, until late in the evening when one of the male guests (a date of one of the male groomsmen) got drunk and decided to hit on the groom's little brother (who was only 14 at the time). A fight ensued and, after the obnoxious drunk was removed, the couple took the microphone to apologise to everyone present for the behaviour of the guest. They were afraid the incident had shed a bad light on homosexuals in general, and it was touching how everyone supported them. (What they didn't realise was that 'drunk and stupid' has nothing to do with sexual orientation.) Seems like the majority of reception problems are caused by drunkenness.

'Ishrugged' USA

Unforeseen hangover

I had a glittering wedding at the Grosvenor House with gorgeous dress, tiara, wonderful food at the wedding dinner, all covered by *Hello!* magazine, etc, but drank oh so much champagne! My huge problem was that I forgot to take any painkillers for my wedding night at Grosvenor House before jetting off on honeymoon to St Lucia the next morning. Consequently my wedding night was marred by my extreme hangover!

My wedding day was the best day of my life apart from when my daughter was born ... just as painful though in a different way!

The problem was not resolved until I got home in the morning where we dropped by briefly to collect gear for the honeymoon and I was reunited with my painkilling tablets! Being a so-called health expert I only usually drink two units per day and don't take tablets. But extreme situations call for extreme remedies and one's wedding day should be a once-in-a-lifetime experience where one might go a bit mad. So be prepared, as the Boy Scouts say!

Advice to all brides: if you're likely to get plastered on your wedding day, take a supply of hangover remedies with you for your wedding night!

Sally Farmiloe-Neville
Hot Gossip UK / Farmingham Productions
www.hotgossip.co.uk
www.sallyfarmiloe.com

Animals at Weddings

I once went to a beautiful wedding in northern France, in a small village near Arras. The whole village turned out for the wedding, including the family's various dogs as well as some of the farmers' herding dogs. It was a lovely touch, especially as the bride and groom are animal lovers, but as you can imagine we did get some snarls and growls while standing around waiting for photographs to be taken. (From the dogs that is, although some of the human guests were displeased at the delay: see the section titled Photography.)

If you have a dog or other pet and want it to be at your wedding, do allow for the fact that the animal is likely to be nervous in such an unfamiliar environment and may not behave too well. In any case, it's a good idea to get someone responsible to look after the animal at all times. And of course, don't forget to check with the officiant and/or owners of the ceremony premises if animals are allowed.

A

Poor pussycat

I decided I fancied a photo of our cat with me in my wedding dress. She was part of my family and therefore it seemed natural to me to have her in the pre-wedding family photos. It was actually the photographer's idea. But on the day there were so many people at the house, the cat just got scared and wanted to get down. She then clawed my neck and drew blood. Blood dripped onto my wedding dress and my neck had big bright red claw marks. This was 20 minutes before we were due to leave for the church.

My dad, who doesn't drink, gave me a neat shot of whisky (to calm me down) the dress was removed and my mum and her team cleaned it as best as they could and blow-dried it with the hair dryer. Ice was put on my neck to take the redness down, then makeup was put on to hide the marks. I was pretty shaken but we made it to church on time. My neck was still a little red and there was a slight stain on the dress. The photographer painted the pictures to hide both.

She was a lovely cat and I wasn't ever mad at her about it. I was mad at myself for trying to have the photo taken. I knew she wasn't happy and I should have said no. Instead, because it was 'in the plan' I let myself get pushed along with it. So my tip is, never mix animals and weddings!

Julie, UK

Best Man and Ushers

The choice of best man is easily as important as, if not more than, that of choosing the maid/matron of honour. To put it crudely, grooms are less likely to be well organised than brides, so it's often down to the best man to ensure that everything runs smoothly.

Never forget that there is a lot more to being a best man than merely making a funny speech. Although the groom's first choice may be his best pal from the pub or his hippy brother who lives in a commune in Thailand, you could be asking for trouble by selecting them. If offence might be caused through not asking such people, give them another key role in the wedding, like reading a poem, making a speech, playing or singing during the evening's entertainment, etc. Then choose a nice, dependable type who knows how to read a wristwatch and won't drop the rings down an open manhole.

Don't forget, too, that many grooms now opt for a best woman – a good friend, sister, cousin, colleague. Much as this may fly in the face of tradition, never forget that women are usually much better organisers than men and tend to get their priorities right ... or at least will have similar priorities to those of the bride!

Ushers aren't so much of a problem, provided they remain sober while ushering people into the ceremony venue and know a) where people should sit and b) where to guide people after the ceremony. This job is normally taken on by the groom's other friends, siblings and other (usually, but not exclusively) male relatives.

Clothes for the best man and ushers have moved on a lot since the traditional days of the dark suit, morning suit or dinner jacket/tuxedo. Although those are still very much in circulation, male attendants can also be booted and suited in lighter colours and different designs. Much depends on the groom's individual preferences, as the best man and ushers' outfits should echo what the groom is wearing. Just bear in mind that it's a lot easier and cheaper to hire morning suits or tuxedos than it is to find six identical sky blue designer suits.

A last word about hired male outfits: don't leave it until the day before the wedding to pick them up from the hirer's premises. If a mistake has been made you have very little time in which to get it put right. I know there are many funny stories about grooms wearing hats several sizes too big which cover their noses and best men in trousers so tight they deliver their speech in a squeaky voice. However I don't imagine you want people remembering your wedding for reasons like that.

Bridal Showers

Bridal showers are essentially a North American notion but I, for one, think they're a terrific idea for us over here in Europe! Essentially they consist of a party for the bride's (mainly female) friends and family, who pre-empt the wedding list and arrive equipped with some incredibly useful and desirable gifts for the bride-to-be.

I, for one, vote for bridal showers to become a part of European wedding culture. How about you?

Bridesmaids, Flower Girls and Pages

Choosing bridesmaids and particularly the maid/matron of honour can be a tough one, especially when your best friend or beloved sister is not the type of person who is well suited to being organised and helpful. Equally if you have two sisters or two very close friends, or one of each, you'll find it hard to choose between them and will be reluctant to make a choice for fear of upsetting whichever doesn't get the job.

B

Unless you want to have a very traditional wedding, or there are restrictions with your religion or culture, don't forget that nowadays it's OK not to stick to the old rules.

Can't choose between your best friend and your sister as maid of honour? Have both. There is no reason whatsoever why you can't have two maids/matrons of honour who share the duties between them. There's also no reason these days why you shouldn't have two best men, or a best woman instead of a best man, or even a man of honour instead of a maid or matron.

If your difficulty of choice is related purely to numbers of candidates, a useful strategy to use is to say 'family only' or 'adults only.'

By shaking up the traditional casting of wedding attendants you may ruffle a few feathers, especially amongst the older members of your family. But as always, do not forget whose wedding it is. What's important is that you have the people nearest and dearest to you with you when you get married – and that in making your choices of who to have you're not obliged to hurt anyone who really matters to you.

Long lost friends

When thinking of who to choose as bridal attendants many brides ask old friends they haven't seen for a long time, for totally understandable senti-mental reasons. However, the reality is that people can change over the years and turn out not to be quite as the bride remembers them. The answer? Get back in touch with your old friend and get to know him or her again before asking them to be a bridal attendant, even if it's long distance via email and telephone. Try to find out what their financial circumstances are; they might not be able to afford to travel to your wedding, never mind pay for the necessary dress or suit. Once you're confident that the friend-ship is still strong and there is no obvious reason why they wouldn't want to be your bridal attendant, ask away.

Disinterested bridesmaids

If you're the bride you could be forgiven for thinking that your bridesmaids and maid/matron of honour aren't as excited about your wedding as you are – especially after the initial rush of adrenalin has passed and you're into the middle phases of the run-up to your wedding. You may even find that it's dif-ficult to get them together for shopping excursions, dress fittings and so on.

B

Although you can't infuse quite the same energy into them that you feel (or not!) it will help a lot if you turn such activities into social activities, tied in with a lunch, dinner, drinks in a wine bar or even a 'girls' night out' at a club. And as always, allow plenty of time before the big day, so you're more likely to find dates that everyone can do.

Maid of (dis)honour

I invited my best friend to be my maid of honour. Though I had given her every available 'how-to' article in the world she still failed to go above and beyond when helping me with the wedding. She did not prepare her speech and winged it and she brought a boyfriend of three days who wore a tank-top to a dinner with my future in-laws two days before the wedding.

Note to self, think about who you ask and let them know how dependent a bride is on the maid of honour's ability to pitch in and be presentable. My sister-in-law ended up helping (she was in the wedding party) and the boyfriend served as fodder for future jokes!!

Tammie Scott, USA

Sometimes you will find that the maid or matron of honour, bridesmaid or best man/woman of your choice just doesn't come up to scratch. Hard though it may seem, it could be that you need to drop the person concerned. Never forget that it's your wedding and you owe it to yourself to ensure that everything possible is done to avoid the day being spoiled. That may mean being a bit ruthless here and there, but it really is worth it.

A disinterested or incapable attendant is just what you don't need. Should you become aware that a key attendant is not up to it, be kind but firm and tell them your feelings. If after an appropriate period they don't improve their attitude and performance, tell them nicely that you want them to be part of your big day, but that you need to get someone else to do the principal honours.

Then, get someone else. You have given the person of your original choice a chance to improve his or her performance and as he/she hasn't, you are perfectly within your rights to ask someone else who can. In fact in some cases where your choice has been based on *who should be asked* rather than *who can do the job*, the original 'askee' might well feel mightily relieved that you're seeking help elsewhere.

Little ones

There's nothing quite so sweet as little girls in beautiful bridesmaids' dresses and little boys in cute pageboy suits, holding hands, smiling beatifically and charming the birds out of the trees. However that's as good as it gets. They can also be tetchy, temperamental, and get a bad attack of stage fright at just the wrong moment.

Choose child attendants with care. If there are children whom you will feel obliged to ask (e.g. your niece or nephew, best friend's daughter or son) and you know they're likely to misbehave or be too shy, it's probably safer to avoid having child attendants altogether.

In the main, though, child attendants are fine as long as you make sure their needs are very well catered for. Usually they love the sense of importance the occasion gives them and take it all very seriously, but they do need to be allowed to chill out afterwards. My son was page at a cousin's wedding when he was 6, along with two other female cousins aged 5 and 7. They looked wonderful together and behaved impeccably throughout the ceremony. But once we got to the reception all three of them were like greyhounds leaping out of their traps. I've got a wonderful picture of them all galloping down the garden of the reception venue, discarding tie, jacket, cummerbund, hair pieces, shoes and various other clothing as they ran – then they shinned up a tree and wouldn't come down for about half an hour.

For ideas on how to occupy them before and after the ceremony, see section titled Children. For some helpful precautions, see sections titled Comfort Breaks and Bridesmaids' Dresses.

Bride's Dress, Hair and Makeup

Here you will be under pressure from various sources, but never forget who is in charge – you. Choose the dress that makes you feel right. Listen to the advice of others by all means, but never forget whose wedding it is.

The home-made option

No matter how talented a seamstress your Auntie is, there can be problems – if only political – connected with letting a close friend or family member make your dress and those of the bridal attendants.

B

Because they're doing you a favour it's very difficult for you to do anything other than fall in with their ideas and schedules, which may not always be as prudent as your own.

If you do go that route be sure you allow what you all consider to be plenty of time for the exercise; and remember that Auntie might think she'll do it faster than she actually can.

Unless it's going to cause untold hurt feelings it's well worth buying your dress from (or getting it made by) the most professional organisation you can afford – one whose reputation for accurate and timely delivery is very important to them. If you're paying them on a strictly business basis you can be stricter about deadlines, and you're far less likely to hear any excuses or encounter hold-ups.

Must yours be white?

No. In fact very few traditional wedding dresses are pure, stark white. Plain white tends to be rather cold, although it can look stunning on some complexions. If you like the idea of the traditional white, but want something a bit more interesting, look at fabrics that are ivory, beige, cream and/or with a hint of pink, blue, aqua, etc.

And if you want to avoid the pale colours altogether, go ahead and wear what colour you like. Apart from a few raised elderly eyebrows, no one these days has a problem with the bride wearing red, yellow or any other colour other than, perhaps, black. The 'white only' rule really is passé now.

Someone else's dress

In your family there may be some pressure for you to wear your mother's or sister's wedding dress, especially if it has become something of a family heirloom. That's fine as long as you want to wear it, but never forget whose wedding it is. If the dress doesn't suit you or you dislike it, get your own.

You may be offered the opportunity to borrow a dress from a relative or friend and provided you like the dress and it works for you, this plan could save you a lot of money. Be careful to establish the ground rules, such as whether you can have the dress altered, when it should be returned, where you should have it cleaned, etc. That way you'll avoid any misunderstandings with the original owner.

Another option that can save a lot of money is to hire a dress. Bear in mind, however, that the dress could be going out a few times in between the day you try it on and the day you pick it up for your own use. If in that time it has acquired a slight stain or some damage, there won't be much time to have it put right.

B

Finally, there is often the opportunity to buy a wedding dress secondhand. If you key **second hand wedding dress** into Google or other search engine, or look up the Wedding Guide in your local *Yellow Pages*, you'll find a number of options. Some say that eBay is another good resource. Charity shops such as those run by Oxfam often carry secondhand wedding dresses that have been worn only once – potentially a valuable source too.

Will you fit into yours?

If I had a pound or a dollar for every bride I've heard of who goes shopping for her wedding dress with every intention of losing a lot of weight for the wedding, I would be rich. Although many brides decide to lose weight in time for their weddings and achieve their objectives, is it really wise to set yourself such a major task alongside all the other major tasks that are involved?

There are many different styles of dress that are very flattering to the fuller figure. Choose one of these and then if you do lose some weight before the wedding – as well you might without even trying, with all you'll have to do – you can have the dress taken in a couple of weeks before the day. I know some brides deliberately buy a dress that's a size or two too small to force themselves into dieting, but this is dangerous. If you don't hit your target there may not be sufficient fabric in the dress to have it let out.

When choosing or commissioning your dress, don't forget that you will be wearing it for several hours, so it should be comfortable. No matter how glamorous you might look in a low cut, heavily boned strapless design, after a few hours of standing and sitting you may well feel like a trussed chicken. You can still look glamorous in a style that does not restrict movement, and that doesn't pinch or grip you too tightly.

Makeup and hair: experiments?

No, no, no. Your wedding day is not the time to experiment with a new look because it might not work. And is this the moment to find out that your presumption was wrong?

B

Because you, as the bride, are the star of the show, despite all other notions you do *not* have to go over the top to be noticed. In fact you don't have to do anything at all to be noticed. It's your day, your show. And of course it's the one time in your life when your own natural beauty and radiance will show through superbly even more than it ever has before.

By all means try out the looks you fancy some time before your wedding and make your decisions on the overall effect then. That way when your wedding day comes around you will know what's going to work, and you and your helpers should be well prepared to implement everything properly.

Shoes: are they comfortable?

No matter how much you may be tempted by some glamorous designer shoes with killer heels, listen to me (the old trout who is so boringly sensible). On your wedding day you will be on your feet for many hours. Don't spoil that by attempting to squeeze your feet into stylish shoes that offer little support and will have you on your knees by the first dance with your new hubby.

Let's face it, if you wear a floor-length dress, the only thing people might notice is the colour of your shoes – not how high or low the heels are. Do yourself a favour and choose a heel height that is truly comfortable for you.

If you will be dancing at your reception and your wedding shoes are of an inappropriate style to allow you to move easily, organise another pair of shoes to be waiting for you at the reception. OK, you probably will prefer to avoid a pair of sensible trainers, but don't let something as silly as shoe style prevent you from salsa-ing the night away in comfort.

Bridesmaids' Dresses

Bridesmaids' dresses are often a source of disagreement in the wedding plan. Not only are there issues involving who pays for the dresses – the bride's family, or each individual bridesmaid? – but also there can be arguments over which design to choose.

One way of solving the latter problem is to specify one colour for the bridesmaids to wear, but provided each dress is of the same colour the design of the dress is up to them. Conversely, you could agree on one design, but each bridesmaid can choose the colour she likes best.

If bridesmaids are expected to pay for their own dresses it's only fair that the bride should agree to a design and colour that will work for the bridesmaids as evening or cocktail dresses later on.

B

When choosing outfits for child attendants don't forget that they tend to grow very quickly! If you're buying their outfits or having them made well ahead of time, allow for plenty of growth room. If the parents are paying for the outfits (and even if you are) it's a kind gesture to choose clothes that the children can wear as party clothes later on. Sailor suits or knickerbockers may look cute on the day, but will not earn the kids many brownie points at a friend's birthday party or the school disco.

Cakes

Along with the 'something borrowed, something blue, etc.' and the throwing of the bride's bouquet, the wedding cake is another of the traditional mainstays of most western weddings. Its origins are said to go back to Roman times or even earlier, and a ceremonial cake pops up in a number of non-western cultures, as well.

It seems the inclusion of fruit and nuts in the cake was originally to represent fertility, or at least the hope of it. In fact in some cultures the cake wasn't so much eaten as squashed up and thrown over the bride to ensure her fertility. Not so good for the expensive hairdo, though.

Why is cutting the cake together such a big deal?

It's said to symbolise your new partnership when you both hold the knife and make the first cut. At many weddings people cheat and have the cake already cut where the couple insert the knife. It may be a little disrespectful to tradition, but it does avoid the embarrassment of the knife slipping or the icing exploding all over the guests. After the first cut is complete and the photographs have been taken, a wise couple will hand over the rest of the carving process to a capable family or staff member. Cutting up a cake is probably not how you want to spend even ten minutes of your wedding day.

C

Who should make yours?

If you're lucky enough to have a friend or relative who is an expert cake-maker and wants to make yours, that's probably a good idea and will save you a fair amount of money. But be warned. Weddings are busy times and if it's a close relative like your mother or your mother-in-law who is making the cake, she will have quite a lot of other stuff to do around the same time as she is making it. This can be distracting. And it only takes an incorrect measurement of flour or sugar to create a last-minute disaster (see Karen's story below.)

Unless you're really on a budget I think it's much safer to opt for a professional cake-maker. If Auntie Margaret has her heart set on making your cake and will be deeply offended if you go elsewhere, try to distract her by saying you wouldn't dream of putting her through all that work and would she like to do a reading at the ceremony, or make a short speech at the reception, instead? That way she will still feel valued, and chances are will probably decline the invitation to speak unless she knows she'll be comfortable with it.

The professional cake-maker does not need to be one of those glossy specialist companies with a whizzing-bow-tie website and a brochure like a coffee table book; your local bakery probably does some lovely designs and will come in at a reasonable cost.

What your local bakery or patisserie does not have, however, is all the other time-consuming aggravation surrounding the organisation of your wedding, particularly in the last couple of weeks when the cake should be made, and it has the resources, staff and time needed to do the job properly. Also the bakery or patisserie has a reputation to keep up and will shift heaven and earth to ensure you are not disappointed.

This is a pretty obvious one, but I'll say it anyway: order your cake in plenty of time. Two or three months before the wedding is about right.

Tips for transporting a cake

If you do have your cake made privately, you or someone else will have to get it to your wedding reception. A couple of tips here. One, if the cake has more than one tier do not assemble it until it's in its final resting place at the reception venue; if you do and there is unscheduled movement during transportation, it could all fall apart. Two, place the boxes containing the cake components on the floor in the passenger footwells of your car (not on the seats or in the cargo area) and pack old sheets or coats or similar around the boxes so they're cushioned should you have to stop suddenly.

C

Why should you have fruitcake if you don't like it?

You don't have to have fruitcake, of course, despite its ancient meaning of fertility. The only advantage of fruitcake is that it keeps very well even if it isn't frozen, although freezing does help retain the moisture and quality. The point? Many couples keep the top tier of the cake to celebrate their first wedding anniversary, or the birth or baptism of their first child. Not so successful a plan if your cake is made of chocolate and ice cream, though.

The other benefit of fruitcake's longevity is when it comes to sending pieces of cake through the post to friends and relatives who were not able to get to the wedding – a common tradition. It may be a little dry by the time it reaches northern Australia from your wedding in London, but it will still be edible. Chances are a piece of sponge or rich Madeira cake would only be fit to serve to wild birds.

However if you both hate fruitcake (I do) then nuts to it, have what you like. It's your wedding!

Their names were (chocolate) mud

Because my brother-in-law was getting married six weeks before us, and they had asked his mother to make one section of their wedding cake, I felt obliged to ask the same. My husband didn't want a traditional cake so instead we opted for a chocolate mud cake that we would serve as dessert.

For several months both myself and my mother-in-law tried out several recipes, but couldn't find one to our satisfaction, until a friend's partner, who was a chef at a leading Sydney restaurant, gave me the perfect recipe. I tried it and we decided it was exactly what we wanted.

I gave the recipe to my mother-in-law who promptly tried it out and then announced that she had changed the quantities of the ingredients because she decided it needed more flour. I don't know if you know much about chocolate mud cake, but that's kind of a key thing! And, since the recipe was exactly what we wanted, we didn't see why she needed to change anything.

As we were having our reception at a restaurant that served amazing food, even at a function, we didn't want the lasting impression for the guests to be an uninteresting, plain cake that you'd have for afternoon tea on a Sunday. So my husband-to-be told his mum that we would organise the cake as it would be less hassle to her, and we asked the restaurant, at short notice, to make the cake for us instead. They did a wonderful job and I'm glad we made the decision. We ended up with a rich chocolate mud cake covered in white chocolate icing. They even managed tiers, though we did have to put it away in the fridge for a while so that it didn't collapse in the heat!

Apparently my mother-in-law was a little offended, but my mum smoothed things over and explained that at our wedding it should be what we want. This is something that still hasn't sunk in, ten years and three children later!

Karen, Sydney, Australia (still happily married, despite the in-laws!)

Cars

The choice of wedding cars is usually listed as one of the key components of any wedding plan. There certainly is no shortage of choice nowadays of anything from old double-decker London buses to stretch Hummer 4WDs that look like giant breeze blocks on wheels.

If you're happy to go along with modern limos and cars you're pretty safe, especially if you use a reputable company that, preferably, has been recommended to you by someone you trust.

Oddball choices, are they reliable?

Many companies offer vintage and other lovely old cars as wedding transport and, frankly, I can't think of anything more romantic than being driven around in a 1935 Bentley with real wood, real leather and all of the Agatha Christie style and panache. However once again reality rears its ugly head. Old cars can break down.

If you hire one of these companies, ensure they provide you with one or even two contingency plans – i.e. if that Bentley conks out on the day, what will they replace it with? If they give you a fuzzy answer, use somebody else. Especially if your wedding is scheduled for a popular month, the company concerned might be tempted by greed and hire out all their vehicles to different weddings on the same day. If one vehicle goes sick, they're stuck. A bigger company probably will have found this one out the hard way earlier on, and is more likely to have appropriate back-up.

Relatives' and friends' own

If someone you know has a nice car and offers to drive you to and from your wedding in it, you'll certainly save some money. However bear in mind that no matter how well intentioned people are, things can still go wrong. If nothing else, you will sleep better in your bed at night knowing that there is a contingency plan in place – even if it is your Mum's hatchback with some white ribbon on it.

C

Disaster car

At a wedding where I was an usher we were just driving back from having ribbons and bows tied to the car for the bridesmaids and ushers when the exhaust fell off. We went round to the local exhaust centre which didn't have the right part in stock but, after much bribery, were able to bodge another part to fit. However, we were now an hour behind schedule.

Got to the church – after most of the guests had arrived – to find that the boot of said car would not open. In the boot were the orders of service, flowers, top hats and various other minor accessories to the ceremony.

Access to the boot was eventually and unceremoniously gained by yanking at the back seat until it gave way and I could crawl through and release the boot catch from the inside.

Tom Crellin, UK

Suitability of cars and other vehicles

You'll often see pictures in local newspapers of couples riding off to their wedding reception on a motorcycle or in a small sports car. That's fine and very romantic and being the cynic that I am, I can't help wondering what happens to the poor bride's dress, train, veil, shoes, hair, makeup and sanity on that journey.

Some great friends of mine got married and decided they would drive from the register office to the reception – a distance of about 5 miles – in the groom's beloved 1960s BMW Isetta Bubble Car. For readers unfamiliar with this vehicle, it's the size of a small bathtub with three wheels, a front opening door and enough room inside for two underweight 12-year-olds. As you can imagine there was a great deal of heaving, grunting and swearing as we squeezed the bride into her seat; not only was she wearing an elaborate, full skirted long dress, but also she was 7 months pregnant with twins. Bad idea.

The moral of this, then, is think ahead. When planning your wedding on a lovely sunny summer day the thought of riding to the reception in a vintage MG sports car with your new hubby at the wheel seems delightful. Remember, though, that on the day it could be raining. If you are dead set on using a vehicle that's less than wedding-dress friendly, have something warmer and drier on standby.

Stretch limos

Most stretch limos are what the motor trade unromantically calls 'cut and shut' vehicles – an ordinary car, van or SUV that has been chopped in half vertically, extra panelling installed to extend it, then all welded up again. Provided that this has been done properly there's no problem, but some 'cut and shut' vehicles have been done on the cheap to an alarmingly poor standard. At best this can make the vehicle unreliable (e.g. the electrics may have been wired back up wrongly) and at worst it can make it downright dangerous.

When hiring a stretch limo choose a reputable company – preferably one that is personally recommended by someone you trust – and avoid the guy around the corner with the 1980s bright purple American stretch parked in his driveway. That might just be a stretch too far...

Caterers

Usually the catering options are as follows.

1. Service provided as part of wedding package at hotel, restaurant, pub, etc.

2. Outside catering company comes in to your venue, hired by you.

3. Catering done by you, family members and friends.

Option 1 is normally pretty safe, but options 2 and 3 can lead to a bit of nail-biting on your part as although the good news is you have more direct control over the food and drink served, you also have the worry of whether it will all hang together on the day.

As for Option 2, the outside catering company, personal recommendation is probably the best way to ensure you steer clear of trouble. Interview companies, ask for references and check them out. Try not to be too heavily influenced by price, because with catering as with so many other things, you tend only to get what you pay for. Particularly if your wedding is taking place during the peak of the 'wedding season,' ask the company what contingency plans they have for staff shortages, etc, and how they handle such a busy workload effectively.

Option 3 can work brilliantly, but you must be able to trust all involved!

Also see section titled Food and Drink.

Children

Should you invite guests' children or not?

C

This is a tricky one. Whether we like it or not weddings are not occasions that children particularly enjoy, because in their eyes the reception, particularly, is just a lot of grownups sitting and standing around eating, drinking and talking.

However for some parents of young children it may be difficult for them to find someone to care for them while the adults attend your wedding, especially if you're all from the same community when most potential baby-sitting adults are fellow wedding guests.

No matter how much you may be pressurised about having children at your wedding, your decision needs to be based on *your* criteria, not those of others. If you can afford to invite them and have someone keep them entertained (see below) that's great, but if you're on a budget or are holding the reception in an unsuitable place, then you're perfectly within your rights to exclude them.

Normally you specify on your wedding invitations just who within a family is invited by itemising the names of each invitee. Some guests can be a bit bullet-proof here though, and bring the children along anyway. To avoid that and make things crystal clear you can include a line on your wedding invitations which says something like 'we're very sorry, but the ceremony and reception can't accommodate children under the age of XX.'

Children involved in second/subsequent marriages

The issue of how to tackle the announcement of your wedding to your children from previous relationships is fairly well documented in other books and websites, and strictly speaking isn't part of my remit in terms of 'wedding worries'. However the backdrop provided by children's attitudes towards future step-families can have a very strong influence on the wedding itself.

Many children harbour a secret or not-so-secret dream that their parents will one day get back together again. The fact that one parent is marrying someone else, therefore, shuts the lid on that particular dream. I haven't been in that position myself, but I understand from those who have that the key here is to encourage such children to talk openly about their feelings. And that's not rocket science; good, open communications usually do go a long way towards healing most rifts and resolving unhappy issues. It's important, too, that you are aware of the fact that the children may be mourning the loss of that dream, even if they are very pleased at the thought of you marrying again. Be sensitive.

If your new partner is well known to and well liked by the children that makes it very much easier. If there are difficulties, ironically the wedding could actually help resolve them, provided that everyone pulls together and the children are deeply involved with the planning and the wedding itself. There's nothing like shared excitement and active teamwork on a positive project to smooth over rough patches within family relationships. Also this can be a useful exercise to help future step-children from both sides to get to know each other better.

Involving children

It's important that you involve your children in the planning and the wedding whether there are any ill feelings or not. You can get them involved with the ceremony itself as attendants, and in many religious services you can be given away by an older child, have an older child as best man, best woman, or maid of honour. This helps them feel involved not only with the wedding, but also with the marriage, which can have helpful long-term consequences.

In some circumstances you can even involve children in the procedures, such as including family vows, or 'parents and children' vows. Even if your wedding is very small and informal, you will probably be allowed to have your children stand with you while the ceremony is conducted.

You can ask them to perform readings during the ceremony, compose and read poems and, if they're musical, have them play something either during the ceremony or at the reception.

Another good idea is to give each child a special 'wedding gift' of value, like a piece of inscribed jewellery or silver *objet d'art*.

On the other hand, it's probably unwise to push children into taking an active part in your wedding if they aren't all that enthusiastic about it. You'll soon find out just how far they want to be involved with some tactful questioning and open discussion.

What matters most is that the children *know* you and your partner want them to be as much a part of your wedding as they want to be. That really does help stop them feeling left out.

Also see the section titled Second Marriages.

Keeping them entertained

Children can get bored and up to mischief during a wedding reception. A good idea is to arrange for some responsible adults to keep them entertained and under supervision so their parents can relax and enjoy the reception. If you can afford to hire a children's entertainer that's great, but two or three capable teenagers will probably do it just as well, and can take turns so they can participate in the wedding festivities too.

Churches, Synagogues and Other Religious Venues

Assuming this is the first marriage for both bride and groom there shouldn't be too many problems in arranging a religious wedding ceremony. Bear in mind that churches, synagogues and other religious venues do get booked up a long way in advance, especially during the peak 'wedding season'.

If you do want a religious wedding ceremony, the religious venue of your choice should be first on the list of who to contact to make a booking. From there on you will be guided by the requirements of your particular religion.

Also see sections titled Civil Partnerships, Inter-faith Weddings and Second Marriages.

Civil Partnerships

How do you go about organising yours?

You organise a civil partnership just as you would a straight wedding to take place in a register office or licensed venue. Probably your first port of call should be your local register office where you'll get the information you need.

As you can imagine, since civil partnerships became law in December 2005 numerous websites and other organisations have sprung up especially to cater for 'gay weddings'. I have no doubt whatsoever that the majority of these organisations are extremely helpful not only in advising you about procedures and other practical aspects of organising the day, but also in answering any questions you may have about the legal and emotional aspects.

To find out more about how to organise your civil partnership, where to find gay-friendly religious ministers, gay-friendly suppliers, etc, key **gay weddings** into Google UK or another UK search engine, or look in the 'Wedding Guide' of your local *Yellow Pages*.

To find out all you need to know about the legal implications of civil partnerships, key **civil partnerships** into Google UK or other UK search engine.

How do you make the announcement to your families?

Obviously, a lot depends here on how far 'out' you are in the first place where your families are concerned. I'm straight, so have no personal experience here, but have many gay friends who advise me that ideally you should get the 'coming out' issue achieved with your families before you announce your civil partnership plans. That makes sense, really.

As civil partnership ceremonies currently may only be conducted by a Registrar in the UK, the issues of who should give one partner away, who should be the best man/woman, etc, do not arise unless you plan such customs into your ceremony deliberately.

However there is nothing to stop you – and everything to be gained by – involving your parents, siblings and children in the ceremony as far as possible. Not only does this make them feel part of your ceremony, but also part of your partnership. And that can be very precious to all concerned.

Is there still disapproval?

Generally speaking, the only areas in which there is still some disapproval of civil partnerships is within religions. At the time I'm writing this it's only Liberal Judaism which has accepted CPs and has published a gay wedding liturgy to be used in its synagogues. Getting a religious blessing in other religions is not necessarily impossible though, and there are many gay-friendly officiants willing to help. As is the case with straight couples, you're not allowed any religious content in the civil ceremony.

What restrictions are there on where and what you do?

In the context of the civil ceremony, the short answer is that there are no restrictions. You are allowed to conduct the ceremony in any venue licensed for civil services, whether gay or straight. You're perfectly entitled to design the ceremony as you wish provided that it has no religious content (see above), but your options are still wide and varied. You can have readings, an exchange of rings, your own personalised vows and pretty well anything else.

Can you go abroad?

Many countries now have civil partnership legislation that's similar to that of the UK, and a civil partnership conducted there will be recognised under UK law. First though, it's important that you check with the embassy or high commission of the country concerned to find out how you stand.

What should you wear?

As is the case with most weddings these days – with the exception of those conducted within stricter religious environs – essentially you can wear whatever you like.

On the other hand, though, a wedding is a special occasion and you may well want to honour it by wearing appropriately formal outfits, and even 'traditional' wedding outfits like bridal gowns and morning suits.

Whatever you choose, let it be an expression of who you are and what matters to you. That's all that counts.

Hers and hers tuxedos
We worked a lesbian wedding once. They solved the problem of bride/bride by one of them wearing a white tuxedo and the other wearing a black tuxedo. The 'bridesmaids' were in white tuxs (two girls, one guy), the 'groomsmen' were in black tuxs (two guys, one girl). During the ceremony (held at a Unitarian Universalist church) they had a female minister, and she said 'You may kiss each other' rather than 'kiss the bride'. It all went very well and was extremely tasteful.

'Ishrugged,' USA

Civil Weddings

Civil weddings – in a register office – are a fairly quick and simple way to get legally married. Usually the only conditions are that you comply with the legal requirements and if you have been married before can provide appropriate documents to prove your previous marriage has been dissolved.

However the ceremonies in these venues tend to be pretty short and sweet, and often do not provide quite the drama and importance you would like to associate with something as important as getting married.

It's helpful to talk to the Registrar and/or his/her staff where you intend to get married, because normally you can add things into the basic ceremony such as poetry readings and other elements. At the time I'm writing this, though, I understand that you are not allowed to include any religious content in a civil ceremony in the UK.

C

For the full range of up-to-date information on the regulations about civil marriage in the UK, go to www.Google.co.uk or other UK search engine and key in **marriage + legalities**, or look up 'Registration of Births, Deaths and Marriages' in your local telephone directory.

Comfort Breaks

Why are they important?

The bottom line with weddings, as with any other form of significant occasion, is that they happen over a substantial amount of time during which the human bladder is expected to cope with anything from minor discomfort to major duress.

Knowing that you are about to experience a wedding ceremony that can last for anything from 10 minutes up to an hour or much more, it really is worth taking precautions to try to avert an inappropriate call of nature. That means not drinking too much for 2–3 hours beforehand. Avoid alcohol and caffeine, as they both can act as diuretics and increase your need to go.

Be especially mindful of this rather unromantic issue where children are concerned. One thing you probably want to avoid is the sound of a little voice piping up with 'Mum, I need a wee' just as you are saying your vows. Ensure that all little ones have had a chance to go before they leave for the ceremony.

Another instance in which you need to be mindful of comfort break needs is during the reception, especially if you're having a sit-down meal. Out of kindness to your guests, you should give them a 5-minute break before the speeches start and warn them appropriately; something your master of ceremonies or best man/woman can do.

C

I once went to a business dinner where the dessert course was swiftly followed by one of the funniest after-dinner speeches I have ever heard, given by that wonderful speaker, Bob 'The Cat' Bevan MBE. For 45 minutes he had everyone in the audience laughing until the tears ran down their faces, and crossing their legs as tightly as they could. No sooner had Bevan sat down than the entire audience leapt up and out of the doors in search of toilets. Had the organisers given us a comfort break before the speaker, we would have enjoyed him even more.

Thirsty work

I was involved with the planning of the wedding and did the table plan, table names, menus, placecards and the most nerve-racking thing – a reading at the church.

The problem was I had a bad chest at the church and spent the whole time fighting not to cough during the whole ceremony. It was a red hot day, no air conditioning and it was being filmed so I was trying not to make a sound.

I had to keep drinking water which made me need the toilet too, so crossing my legs and drinking, while miming to the hymns, as if I'd started to speak or sing I would have coughed. Nightmare – but speech luckily went okay.

Faye Cassidy, UK

Confetti

There's not much to say about confetti, except for the fact that many wedding venues – both religious and social – hate it! It makes a terrible mess and is a so-and-so to clean up afterwards, especially if it has been raining. Some venues also dislike rice, flower petals and other gentle missiles for the same reason.

Before you allow anyone in the wedding party to throw confetti, make sure you ask the venue how they feel about it first, otherwise you could find yourself with a hefty cleaning bill that you weren't expecting.

Decorations

See section titled Flowers.

Destination Weddings

If you peruse the pages of glitzy feel-good magazines (I do while waiting for my son's school bus) you'll often see spreads of celebrities idyllically marrying their sweethearts on an exotic beach in some tropical tax haven. Ah, wouldn't it be wonderful…

Then I think again. If I have just spent £50 on a pedicure do I really want to traipse barefoot through burning sand to be married under a palm tree? Do I really think I can wear a full length satin gown, elaborate hairdo and full makeup in 40°C heat and look cool and glamorous after the first three minutes? Never mind; I'm just a pragmatic old Taurean.

Getting married abroad is becoming quite popular for a number of reasons – and not just because you can combine wedding and honeymoon in one hit.

What's the point?

The first point is a huge reduction in hassle factor. Particularly if you use one of the numerous specialist agencies which have sprung up in recent times (just key **destination weddings** into Google or other search engine, or look up the Wedding Guide in your local *Yellow Pages*) virtually all you do is pick the time and place, pay for it, and turn up. Of course you can design your own bespoke wedding abroad too. But at least with this option you can choose how much involvement you take on.

Interestingly enough, despite the air fares and hotel costs, a wedding abroad can turn out to be much less expensive than a wedding at home, largely because you don't have the expense of a lavish reception for large numbers of people. Because most of the old traditions become irrelevant when you go abroad, the cost can be spread more comfortably across the whole family, even with everyone paying their own way. As for who you invite, you can be very picky indeed and select only those you really want to share the day with, although this can have disadvantages too (see below).

Other attractions

Alternatively you can just disappear on your own and tell everyone about it afterwards (also see the section title Elopement). Some friends of mine did that as part of their annual holiday in Barbados one Christmas; it was just them and their three sons. They sprang a double surprise on us all when they got back because we all thought they were married already! When I asked the new bride why she had sneaked off secretly she said, 'I couldn't have stood the pain of my mother organising a wedding in this country.'

Another indisputable attraction is the glamour element. OK, the sandy beach may not be my idea of perfection, but the thought of getting married in a beautiful location like Venice or East Africa does sound wonderful. There's just an added spark you can't get at home.

What are the problems?

Well, to begin with you won't be in control of your wedding in the same way that you would be at home. No matter how carefully you liaise with the venue and local organisers, you're still operating by remote control to an extent and are reliant on their carrying out your wishes. With a wedding at home, you can be much more 'hands on'.

The whole issue of who accompanies you can be tricky, too. The people who matter most to you may not be able to afford the money and time to travel to your destination, and you may not be able to afford to pay for their flights and accommodation. Then, because your guest list will be pretty short, you risk offending some people who have been left off it. That applies, too, if just the two of you go; not only will you have to invite someone you don't know to be your witness at the ceremony, but also you may find your immediate families feel cheated at having been left out of it.

To an extent that problem can be remedied if you have a good party when you get back. Although that will cost some money to put together you won't be obliged to spend on the traditional and costly elements like the cake, flowers, lavish entertainment, etc. Your party can be anything you want from dinner in a restaurant with everyone paying for themselves, to a casual barbecue or meet-up in your favourite pub.

What about the weather?

Don't be fooled into thinking that exotic locations have year-round hot sunshine. I got an email last September from a friend who lives near Mombasa, Kenya, saying that she was indoors wearing jeans and two sweaters while outdoors it was pouring with rain, accompanied by a howling gale.

Whilst it may be hot in Caribbean locations during the months of June, July, and August there is often very high humidity, which makes outdoor existence extremely sweaty and uncomfortable – not to mention having a disastrous effect on recently-straightened hair. If you wait until a little later in the season you get not only heat and humidity but also gales and hurricanes. And so on.

Naturally you will do your homework to find out all you can about the destination of your choice. Beware cut-price packages and 'off-season' deals; remember the old adage that if you pay peanuts you get monkeys. Discounted deals are usually discounted for a reason you would rather not find out about the hard way – like impending monsoons, a half-built or ancient hotel, thundering jet planes landing a hundred metres away, or a resort's recent bout of food poisoning that affected 200 guests.

In non-tropical destinations like European capital cities the weather is not necessarily as much of an issue, but it would still make sense to pick a time of year when your chances of a bit of sun and warmth are higher than average. Even Paris, Amsterdam, Venice, Florence and Rome are pretty dull and miserable in November.

Directions and Parking

No matter how careful you have been to provide your guests with directions on how to get from the wedding ceremony to the reception, some people will have forgotten to bring them along. If the reception is within shouting distance of the ceremony venue – or you have laid on transport for everyone – then there isn't a problem. But if people have to get into their cars and find the reception, have someone standing in an appropriate place (e.g. the exit of the wedding ceremony venue or the entrance to the car park) with copies of the directions on paper, handing them out to whoever needs them. It's probably useful to include the full address and postcode of the reception venue in case people want to use an in-car GPS system.

Double Weddings

What's the point?

Double weddings aren't very fashionable these days, but can offer considerable advantages. First of all they are a lovely idea where two couples who are close friends, or where there are two siblings, can share this fantastic experience together. The other, more down-to-earth reason is that there can be considerable cost savings.

In the case of two couples who share many of the same friends and family members, spreading the cost – particularly of the reception – makes the whole thing more affordable. It also mean that because of the economies that are possible, the two couples together can afford what may be a somewhat more lavish wedding than if they were picking up the tab by themselves.

What are the realities?

Obviously if you're a bride who wants to be the sole star of the day, a double wedding is not for you.

The issue of having two brides and their families organising the whole thing can jump in one of two directions. If the two brides get along very well they will share the chores of wedding planning and preparation and so relieve some of the burden and stress associated with doing it on their own. However by the same token, should there be disagreements between the brides and/or their families, you double the aggravation.

The takeout message here is, only go for a double wedding if you know both brides can work harmoniously together – and under pressure, too. Don't forget that you will have to agree on everything from the design of the invitations to the colour schemes of the flowers to the bridesmaids' dresses to the choice of menu for the reception. You need to be pretty well in tune with the other person to achieve that.

Can they happen anywhere?

D

In theory the answer is yes, but in practice some officiants may not be keen on the idea. Some religions may not permit double weddings at all. Because double weddings tend to involve a larger crowd of people than the single variety, some churches, register offices and other wedding ceremony venues may not be big enough.

If you want to have a double wedding it's sensible to check with your intended officiant and venue very early on in the planning process a) to allow plenty of time for them to prepare for it and b) to save you wasting time on planning if the answer is no.

Who does what?

When two sisters are the brides, normally their father (or whoever would perform that role) walks the older bride up the aisle and a brother or other close male relative does the honours for the younger sister. The father gives both sisters away in the ceremony, though, and if everyone prefers, he also can walk both girls up the aisle with one on each arm.

To avoid the ceremony looking like a performance of the local choral society, it's a good idea for the brides to share the bridesmaids. You need two best men/women, though, and you could probably have a maid or matron of honour each.

As far as I can ascertain there are no existing customs regarding the speeches at double weddings, so logic should prevail. Obviously in the case of two sisters the father of the bride or whoever is performing that role can manage with just the one speech, appropriately shared between the two brides. However unless the grooms are brothers, you will probably want to have two best men/women speeches. As the grooms will want to speak and possibly the brides as well, here more than anywhere it's important to keep the speeches short.

Also see the section titled Speeches.

Who goes first?

The usual plan is that the older of the two brides has her name uppermost on the wedding invitations, goes into the church first, and her family take precedence in the seating arrangements over the family of the younger bride (assuming they're not sisters). However there are no hard and fast rules about this and you're perfectly entitled to handle this whichever way you want.

D

You may want to choose a wedding ceremony venue with an aisle wide enough that both brides and their male escorts can walk up together, and both couples can walk back down together after the ceremony.

Dress Code

If you want to specify a dress code on your wedding invitations by all means do so, but be aware that not everyone can afford to hire morning suits, tuxedos/dinner jackets, etc, or even fancy dress costumes for that matter.

Sometimes, obviously, dress code can be related to religious or cultural reasons and in that case it's much kinder to invited guests to warn them about it beforehand, so they're not embarrassed or wrong-footed when they arrive at your wedding.

If you do have a choice, though, don't lose sight of what really matters – your guests' presence at your wedding, no matter how they're dressed!

Elopement

Although we no longer see many cases of passionate teenage couples racing to Gretna Green hotly pursued by their furious families, there are reasons why you might want to elope.

Family disapproval can still be an issue and often the thought of dealing with antagonistic parents and other family members can make you decide to disappear and tie the knot – then tell them afterwards, stand back and watch the explosions, knowing there's nothing they can do about it. Whatever the disapproval is about – personalities, social backgrounds, religions, cultures, ethnic backgrounds, etc – elopement sometimes seems to be the only way forward, if discussion and communication fail.

It's not just antagonism that can cause a desire to elope, either. It can also be the thought of having your families climb all over the wedding plans, guest lists and reception arrangements, running the whole event without giving you the chance to do more than choose your dress and get your hair done, and claiming ownership of the whole thing so you feel you're merely a second-division participant.

My parents eloped for exactly that reason. Although I wasn't there at the time I know from their recollections how it feels to do it, and how it feels to have to clean up the hurt and hostility afterwards. Whatever the reasons for eloping, you know you will see some fireworks on your return and genuinely will have upset a number of people you care about – even if they have opposed your marriage. That's the price you pay. However once some time has passed and you have, perhaps, held one or two post-wedding celebrations, in many cases things get better – especially when the first grandchild comes along.

The regulations, England and Wales

Both parties must be over 16. If under 18 you must have written permission to marry from an appropriate parent or guardian. Obviously you must not be closely related; you must be acting of your own free will, and be able to understand the full implications of the ceremony.

The regulations, Scotland

As above, but in Scotland you *do not* need to have written permission if one or both of you is under 18. This is why Scotland has always been the favoured place for teen elopements. Another reason why it's popular for all elopements is that it's the only country in the UK where you do not need to be 'resident' in the district for a given time prior to getting married there.

For the full range of up-to-date information on the regulations about marriage in the UK, go to www.Google.co.uk or other UK search engine and key in **marriage + legalities**, or look up Registration of Births, Deaths and Marriages in your local telephone directory.

Entertainment

Although barn dances and other themed entertainment are very popular for wedding receptions (see Sue Malleson's contribution,) wedding guests do not always appreciate the enforcement of participation. It's fine to jolly people along a bit as they may feel a bit shy to start with, but don't chase them on to the dance floor with a baseball bat, and don't allow the entertainment organisers to do it either. Accept that some people really do prefer just to sit and watch.

Take your partner

As a barn dance MC I've officiated over the evening entertainment at hundreds of weddings.

The main thing to go wrong with these has been timing. All bands who 'do' weddings are accustomed to turning up and having to sit around sometimes for hours, while the rest of the proceedings grind along. This sometimes results in timings so awry that the evening's events barely get going before the bride and groom leave or the event has to close.

So my advice to anyone planning a wedding is to add in some time between the end of the reception and the evening entertainment. Meals always take longer to serve than the caterers will admit in my experience. So if you've added in half an hour to clear tables, move them and arrange the room for the evening's dancing, add another half hour, because you'll likely need it.

As a barn dance MC – and I'm sure it is the same for any band – the way to make things move smoothly during post-reception entertainment is to plan them as meticulously as you plan the earlier part of the day. Have one person responsible for the evening, who knows whether or not the bride and groom want to do a first dance, what it will be, what music they want, whether they want people to join in after a few bars or dance for five minutes on their own. What Auntie Doris thinks the bride and groom want to do is not always what they would wish!

The time that the bride and groom leave – if they do – must be agreed in advance, and what time the event finishes. It is also necessary to ensure that someone has the money to pay the band. That person needs to be sober (so the best man is not always the obvious choice), needs to know when any food will be served, when any cakes will be cut, when any uncles might want to sing (and indeed if the bride and groom wish that). There is often pressure on a band to allow members of the party to play instruments, take the microphone and sing, etc. The more drunk the party is, the more likely this is to happen. So the person in charge must know these rules and tell the band, so that they can be strictly enforced. Same thing goes for impromptu speeches. I know a dreadful story about a (I think best) man who when absolutely drunk at a wedding which a folk band were playing for alluded to an intended and specific sexual practice of the groom's. I wasn't there but one of the musicians who was told me about it. Control is everything. The more control there is, the less likely impromptu theatrical acts are to disrupt or cause embarrassment.

Sue Malleson
Taurus Public Relations, UK
www.tauruspr.co.uk

With a song in your heart

When we got married 15 years ago we had been sneaking off to ballroom dancing classes for weeks without anyone knowing. You see, my wife's parents were very accomplished on the dance floor and we wanted to surprise everyone.

Even though we asked the DJ for something appropriate we couldn't legislate for what followed.

We were called up onto the dance floor and made ourselves ready. The opening bars of the music started, we set off on our waltz – all was going well.

Then we recognised the lyrics – it was 'It's raining in my heart'.

So we duly waltzed over to the DJ and asked for something more appropriate. The music was changed, off we went again.

Then we realised he was playing 'You've lost that loving feeling'.

At this point my brother (who just happened to be a DJ as well) stormed across the dance floor and threatened the hapless man with the option of an album being placed you know where!

Anyway, the music was changed for something suitable – but the funny thing is neither my wife nor I nor any of the guests can remember what it was!

When we got back from the honeymoon we found out that his wife of 25+ years had left him the day before our wedding and he was feeling sorry for himself.

So the moral of the story is make sure you choose the music and make sure the DJ has a copy of it!

David Long,
ClikOnMarketing.com, UK
www.clikonmarketing.com

Music of your choice

Music was to play through the receiving of the guests by the wedding party. I had spent a lot of time finding and recording medieval music for this. I had a friend doing the music, but the wedding hostess at the facility thought she knew best and turned it off. I couldn't get anyone to correct the situation (I didn't want to ask one of the guests or leave the line), and it has bothered me to this day.

'Kikonie', USA

Ex-Partners

There's a big difference between telling your ex that you're getting married (or married again) and actually inviting him or her to your wedding. In the former category there are some moral obligations, but in the latter category it's entirely up to you.

Tell them or not?

No matter how estranged you are from the other parent of your child or children it's only right that you should tell them if you're getting married. In any case your children will know (see section titled Children) and unless they're estranged from their other parent, they are bound to mention it.

This is fair not only because of the change that will take place in your life, but also because of the relationship that your child or children will have with your new spouse.

If you don't have children with your ex then whether you tell him/her or not is entirely dependent on how well you get on with him/her now. You're under no obligation, but unless you absolutely hate each other it's courteous to let him/her know.

Invite them or not?

This is a big one. Nowadays it's very fashionable to have 'blended families' where current partners and former partners all get along as one big happy unit, and provided their feelings are genuine that can provide many benefits for all – especially children. But sometimes I wonder just how genuine those 'happy family' feelings really are. No matter how civilised a break-up has been, in my view usually there is still a bit of lingering baggage. And even if there's just a tiny bit, do you really want that at your wedding?

The issue of whether it's good for your children to have their other parent (your ex) at your wedding is another hot potato. Ostensibly it may seem very grownup and mature to mix everyone together, but some experts believe that it can be confusing, especially for younger children. The idea is that it's better for the children to acknowledge you and your new spouse as an item without the added complication of your ex being around – especially if the children might be inclined to draw comparisons.

If you do invite your ex, make sure you invite their current partner or a 'date' as well, to even things up. If you're doing a sit-down meal it's a good idea to ensure they are placed with people they already know, if possible. And be tactful; don't spend too much time chatting or dancing with your ex and don't rub your new spouse's nose in it by introducing your ex as such. It's better to describe them as an old friend, or as your children's Mum or Dad.

Sticking his nose in

I particularly enjoyed a wedding I went to where the bride had invited an ex-boyfriend. He spent much of the reception making snide comments and generally unnecessarily dishonourable remarks ... that is until the groom took him outside and smacked him very, very hard. I heard that his nose was broken, but I can't be sure since, for some reason, he didn't come back inside.

Dom Pannell, UK

What about their parents?

Once again, if you and your ex have children together then it's courteous to tell your ex's parents that you're getting married again. You do not have to invite them to the wedding, but if you're still on good terms with them, if they approve of your marriage, and if they're close to your children, there's no reason why they shouldn't be invited.

Fathers

Although we live in an age of gender-equality this section really is more about the father of the bride than it is about the groom's Dad. This is a time when many brides will suddenly notice that dear old Dad has gone a bit sulky or quiet, and will wonder what the trouble is – if they have upset him, or done something wrong.

Basically the problem is that he is a bit jealous, and a bit saddened. Jealous because he feels he is 'losing' his little girl to 'another man,' and saddened by the thought that he is being made to move over and no longer be the most important man in your life. And that's likely to be lurking underneath all the goodwill and bravado. It doesn't matter how much he likes your fiancé and how much he may be looking forward to golfing weekends with his son-in-law and how much eventually he wants to be a Grandad. He still feels a bit jilted. And suddenly he feels old, especially if you're the first among your siblings to get married.

Fathers also like to feel in control of things, and the thought that their little girl is getting married and will be emotionally as well as practically independent may introduce an element of insecurity. He's not the boss of the family any more. This problem lurks behind many examples of fathers of the bride who try to use money as control mechanism, where paying for the wedding is concerned.

Unusual behaviour

Fathers may also go into denial, and stay aloof from the wedding preparations, pretending not to care. They may laugh at all the fuss that's going on, or complain that the house is being turned upside down and they can't find anything. They may project their anxiety into the father-of-the-bride speech, and fret and worry themselves silly over it.

Whatever happens, it's important to realise that if your Dad is behaving a bit strangely, he probably has good reasons for it – essentially, because he loves you very much. I know this is hardly a time when brides need a prima donna to cater to, but try to spend as much time with your Dad as you can, and reassure him that you'll always be his little girl. He may brush you off and poo-poo your concern – men in our industrialised society are not meant to show emotion – but deep down he will feel reassured and comforted.

Who gives you away?

Not all father–daughter relationships are sweetness and light and sometimes a bride will not want her birth father to give her away at all.

If there is any concern over whether you should be given away by your father or step-father, birth father or adoptive father, etc, don't feel obliged to make a decision in favour of one or the other.

You can also choose to be given away by your mother, sister or brother, or to not be given away at all – you walk in with your groom, or on your own, and that's it. In many cultures and religions this is perfectly acceptable and goes a long way towards defusing arguments.

Estranged fathers

Further to what I said in the paragraphs above, don't feel obliged to involve your father in the wedding preparations or the ceremony if he hasn't been around for years and hasn't contributed to your welfare. Many people say that blood is thicker than water and the fact that someone is a close relation should take priority for major family occasions like weddings. I say that's nonsense in this case.

What matters is your happiness, that of your partner, and the success of your wedding. Estranged fathers do sometimes emerge from the shadows for big celebrations like this, for their own reasons. Don't be intimidated if that happens to you. Make your decisions based on who you want to be there, give you away, be in the receiving line at the reception, and make the speech. It's your day.

Finances and Budgeting

Ah, that filthy five-letter word: m-o-n-e-y.

At the time I'm writing this (late 2006) the average spend on a wedding in the UK is just under £20,000. That is serious money to all but a few of us, and well beyond the means of quite a few of us too.

One good thing that has happened in recent times which helps ease the strain of wedding costs is the fact that etiquette on who pays for what has relaxed considerably. In the bad old days the bride's family got stuck paying for nearly everything. A father of several daughters would have to save for years and even then virtually bankrupt himself if he was to 'marry off his daughters in style'.

F

Now, thankfully, people are a lot more realistic and financing a wedding is usually shared across the two families and the bride and groom themselves. Not only does this spread the financial load, but also it evens out the politics; if he who pays the piper calls the tune, at least with this arrangement there is a reasonable number of payers. The resulting financial parity makes it a lot more difficult for any individual to get bossy, and it's much easier to run the whole show democratically.

No matter how much money you have available it makes a great deal of sense to set a budget at the outset and stick to it as far as possible. It's also sensible to set aside a contingency fund of, say, ten or 15 per cent of the total in case of unforeseen expenses and emergencies.

How to prioritise

There is lots of helpful information on wedding finances in books and on the internet (key **wedding finance** into Google or other search engine, or look up the Wedding Guide in your local *Yellow Pages*) so I won't go on about it at length here.

Particularly if you're short of money, prioritising the elements of your wedding can make budgeting a whole lot easier. Start with a 'must have' list of essentials like ceremony venue, licences, fees, dress, reception venue, cake, etc.

Continue with a 'should haves' list to include elements like hired cars or other transport, entertainment for the reception, etc, and finish with a 'nice to haves' list of luxury items, silver service sit-down meal, pretty place gifts for guests, live band, exotic honeymoon and so on.

These three lists should make it easier to plan your spend and to ensure enough is allocated to the essentials.

Wrong priorities

One thing that always struck me was the weddings we did where the whole thing was on a shoestring budget. Weddings are so expensive, and often there's no money to create the fairytale so many women dream about as little girls. One wedding that was done badly sticks out in my mind. They shelled out the rather large amount of money for the DJ service, and paid extra to have me videotape, but the dinner consisted of Little Caesar's pizza and a keg of beer. It was held in a hall so cheap it could have been the backroom of a poolhall. The bride wore a huge, poofy, flouncy gown, but there were no flowers or decorations of any kind. It was horrible. No one seemed happy – except later in the evening when everyone was getting drunk.

Another wedding sticks out in my mind that was done well on little money. (They still shelled out money for the DJ and videotaping service, but they had priorities.) The dinner consisted of a sort of potluck from the bride's rather large family – everyone brought a dish to pass, but there seemed to have been a plan involved, so they didn't end up with four salads and no main course. The hall was inexpensive, but tasteful. The bride wore a simple white evening dress and had done her hair herself. She looked amazing. The hall was decorated with the bridesmaids' bouquets as centrepieces on the main tables, and the other centrepieces were glass bowls – each one with a goldfish in it. Add a little sparkly confetti and the place shined. Everyone was so happy.

'Ishrugged', USA

Parents are being domineering

When the parents are paying for the lion's share of the wedding they can sometimes become a bit too pushy and undervalue what you want, in favour of what they think you should have. Money does have a way of talking here as it does everywhere else. But even if you aren't paying anything towards the wedding it is still your day. Obviously some give and take makes sense, but if things go too far in a direction that's wrong for you, threaten to elope. That often brings them to their senses…

Think about your guests

If by any chance yours is to be one of two or more weddings in one family, community or group of friends, it can mean everyone has to find quite a lot of money in a short timeframe. Not only do they need to buy gifts for you and the others getting married, but also the women are likely to want to wear a different outfit to each wedding! Try to avoid setting your wedding date too close to that of another family member, friend or neighbour who is likely to be inviting many of the same guests.

Ways of saving

If you're short of money you can't beat a bit of 'thinking outside the box', as the cliché goes. For starters, provided most of your guests can be a bit flexible on dates and times, you'll get some much cheaper deals from wedding venues if you book on a weekday, and/or in the morning to early afternoon.

You don't have to offer everyone a lavish meal; see the section titled Food and Drink.

F

DIY food of love

It was 1980, we were on a low budget, but wanted to have a wedding that involved both our families. Not being particularly religious at the time we originally decided on a registry office followed by a fairly informal reception, keeping the numbers low in the interests of cost. This failed to take into account my future father-in-law's six siblings, all of whom lived locally and insisted on coming. Once a number of our friends had been added in what started out as an intimate gathering of some 20-30 people had mushroomed to over 70. We had not reckoned on the capacity of Chippenham Registry Office which seated 50 at the most. It was standing room only, with flustered registrars and others bringing in spare chairs to accommodate the influx.

Owing to the budgetary restrictions we decided caterers were out of the question and, apart from a couple of welcome contributions from Sandra's uncle, who was a butcher, and my mother who had developed an awesome ability to make wedding cakes, we prepared all the food ourselves in the days leading up to the wedding. How we managed to prepare and store enough food for 70 people in a tiny council house kitchen in the middle of a hot August I do not know, but we did.

We did most of the cooking late at night to avoid the heat and I have always maintained that if your relationship can withstand cooking quiches at 2 o'clock in the morning together in a tiny kitchen then it can withstand a lot.

Nick and Sandra, UK

As for the number of guests, you'll find it's probably cheaper overall to have a small wedding – family and close friends only – and then have a larger party some time later, maybe when you get back from honeymoon. The thing about parties as opposed to wedding receptions is that people's expectations are not aimed so high! You can even get away with asking people to contribute drink and food at a party, whereas to do so for a wedding reception looks a bit mean.

Reception venues

Rather than hiring a wedding reception venue, look around your family and friends and see if anyone has a largish house you can borrow. Of course you will have to compensate them for any damage, but they may well let you have the place for free. Equally, you may find it cheaper to put up a marquee in your own or someone else's garden, but this can still be quite expensive by the time it has been erected, equipped, decorated, heated, and outside catering has been brought in.

Restaurants are useful places to seek good value for a reception. Particularly if you choose an off-peak day – and/or lunch – you may find they will give you an extremely sensible per-head price. With a restaurant reception usually you can still choose whether to have a buffet or a served meal, and you can get away with asking guests to buy their own wine – perhaps just providing a sparkling wine for the speeches and toasts.

Food and drink

Talking of sparkling wine, forget the expensive champagne. These days it's seen as pretty 'cool' to have a decent sparkling white wine from Spain or Italy instead, at a fraction of the cost per bottle. Depending on the venue you choose for the reception it may be worth your while to take a 'booze cruise' to continental Europe to buy your supplies. However bear in mind that many venues will charge you corkage if you bring your own alcoholic drink.

Another cute money-saving idea is one that comes from across the pond in the US; it's called a 'potluck reception'. The idea is that instead of bringing a wedding gift, guests bring a dish of food. You can set the theme if you want, or ask them to get in touch with you to discuss what they can bring. I've never tried that but it strikes me as a nice idea!

Clothing

Then there are the more obvious ways of cutting back on costs, like hiring a wedding dress (see section titled Bride's Dress, Hair and Makeup) or even buying one secondhand; key **secondhand wedding dresses** into Google UK or other UK search engine for sources, or look up the Wedding Guide in your local *Yellow Pages*.

Flower Girls

See sections titled Bridesmaids, Flower Girls and Pages, and Children.

Flowers

If you have a friend or relative who is good at arranging flowers and offers to do yours for you, it can be very tempting to accept. Not only will you be pleasing the person concerned, but also you will be saving a lot of money on professionals.

Trouble is, you could also be lining yourself up for problems. Well meaning amateurs often can do an excellent job. Often, too, they can underestimate the work involved with doing wedding flowers and find themselves utterly overwhelmed.

We all know how perishable flowers can be, obliging those who arrange them to work very fast and at the last minute, too. When faced with turning around flowers for the ceremony, the reception, the bridal bouquet, the bridesmaids' bouquets, the buttonholes for the guys, corsages for the mums, table decorations, etc, etc, it's enough to make anyone other than the most hardened of professionals burst into tears.

This is not something you want to discover the hard way, when it's too late to take remedial action. But feelings can be hurt if you turn down the offer of amateur help.

Solution? Get your amateur flower expert to help you and the florist 'design' your floral arrangements and decorations. Contrary to expectations, the amateur concerned might even be flattered that you have elevated him or her to 'designer' status. That solves his or her problem, and yours – the amateur feels appreciated and the professionals (who know and can handle the extent of what's needed) do the work.

What about the wedding before yours?

You will often find that churches and other places of worship as well as secular wedding venues get heavily booked up in the spring and summer months, with one wedding after another taking place on the same day.

This can present problems if you want to get yourself or your florist into the ceremony venue to do the flowers prior to your wedding.

One solution to this is to contact the other couples getting married on the same day in the same place, get together with them, agree on a floral scheme you all like, and share the cost. Not only will this solve the practical problem, but also it will save you all quite a lot of money.

Food and Drink

Choosing menus and drinks for your buffet or sit-down wedding meal is not easy. Many couples, though conscious of how varied their guests' tastes in food might be, desperately seek to avoid the 'rubber chicken' type of dull, dreary menu that so often is chosen by large groups for precisely that reason.

There are two points I would make here. One is remember whose wedding it is; pick a menu that will please you and your immediate family and friends. Don't feel obliged to choose something you happen to hate, just because it's widely acceptable to others. The second, is that there need not be more than a few definite no-nos unless your religion or culture has specific rules. The following points should, if observed, satisfy most guests at a modern wedding.

- No pork; some religions don't allow it.

- No shellfish; some religions don't allow it, and many people have shellfish allergies.

- Include a vegetarian alternative to starter and main course.

- Avoid very heavily spiced food unless there are cooler alternatives available.

- Avoid alcohol, obviously, if your religion does not allow it.

- If alcohol is permitted ensure you offer plenty of non-alcoholic drinks for those who prefer them and/or are driving.

Sit-down meals

Sit-down meals are often favoured by families and certainly offer guests a more substantial option, but these meals do have their problems. Not only are you obliged to arrange seating plans for sit-down meals (see section titled Seating Plans), but also the meal concerned is more difficult to arrange.

Many families send out menus with the wedding invitations, asking guests to specify what choice they would like from a selection of options. The returns from this exercise are particularly helpful because they will tell you and your caterers what should be allowed for across conventional tastes, vegetarian options, religiously-orientated options, etc. With large wedding receptions, accommodating everyone's whims can be quite a daunting task, but most wedding caterers are used to that and can cope.

Buffet-style meals

Although less formal, buffet-style meals probably are the preferable option when you have an eclectic mix of guests. With this format you avoid the extra fiddle-factor of asking people to choose their menus beforehand, or the need for you to make painful choices of what to serve at a sit-down dinner. Here you can offer a far wider selection of dishes amongst which nearly everyone will find something they like. The preparation and serving of a buffet meal is also simpler (and therefore should be cheaper) than a sit-down meal for a large number of guests.

F

Barbecues

These are a popular choice for summer weddings, but remember that weather can be an issue here, especially in the good old UK. Most professional venues will allow for the possibility of wet weather, but if you do your reception at home or in another private place, find a way to get the barbecue devices under (non-inflammable) cover if the need arises. The other important thing to remember about barbecues is that the classic foods we cook on them here in the UK are not normally vegetarian-friendly, and are probably not religion-friendly for a multi-cultural guest list. That's not the end of the world though. Within the barbecue choices you can include some delicious veggie kebabs and other things. Key **vegetarian barbecue recipes** into Google or other search engine for some tasty ideas.

Other options

Why stick to traditional meals?

You can take a leaf out of the North Americans' book and do a wedding brunch ... a meal I dearly love and am known to stuff myself with when over on the west side of The Pond. This is especially useful if you want to save money by having a morning wedding – in the UK it's not a particularly popular time, hence lower costs. Brunch can be anything from croissants and scrambled eggs to steak dinners with vegetables and gravy – in fact, whatever you fancy. What distinguishes brunch from other meals is that it (in theory) should be an amalgam of breakfast and lunch, and it takes place somewhere between mid to late morning and around 2pm.

Another wedding feast alternative – which also saves on cost – is afternoon tea. Here you can go ballistic with dainty sandwiches, gorgeous little cakes, scones with clotted cream and delicious preserves, all of which lead nicely up to the wedding cake.

Then, of course, you have the option of doing a reception that consists of drinks and canapés only. This can save a lot of money, but can also seem a bit tight-fisted. There is a way around this, though. A great friend of mine who used to organise drinks parties for corporate clients came up with the brilliant idea of serving a range of canapés which mirror a four-course meal. In other words the first trays of canapés consisted of fish and seafood based titbits plus crudités and dips, bits of melon and parma ham, etc. The next round consisted of canapés based on roasted meats, roasted vegetables and other ideas cribbed from main courses. Then followed canapés which were all sweet – fruit, chocolate, cheesecake and other such delicacies. Finally there was a round of cheese-based tasties. Yum, yum. People felt they had eaten a four-course meal at a fraction of the cost of serving them one.

A Korwedian-American reception

When Carrie, the Korean, and Brian, the Swede, wanted to throw a classy wedding reception celebrating their distinct cultures, what did they do? They persuaded their two wild and crazy moms to prepare ethnic food for 120 guests.

The menu was a celebration of two distinctly different cultures. Korean food is highly spiced and very colourful. Swedish food is mostly white, bordering on bland. To survive Korean food, most people need antacids and all people need breath mints. Korean food yells stinkily; Swedish food whispers nonstinkily.

Carrie selected her favorite Korean dishes: jahb chae (a noodle and vegetable dish with marinated beef), bulgogi (marinated grilled beef), fried rice, kimchi (a highly spiced pickled cabbage). Brian selected his: Swedish meatballs and sausage, Jannsons frestelse (translated means Jansson's temptation which for Swedes is apparently potatoes) and pickled herring. We added Thai chicken wings, a Thai salad, fresh fruit kabobs, cheese trays and an array of freshly baked breads.

The cake was pure American: chocolate with a butter cream frosting. Since most Minnesotans are unfamiliar with Korean food we included signs naming and describing the various dishes, warning those people with sensitive palates.

Personally, I was hoping that the combination of kimchi and herring would dissuade guests from staying too long, drinking too much wine, and procreating potential eighth graders. As Mother of the Bride, I was downright exhausted.

The food and wine disappeared and guests partied until the wee morning hours. It wouldn't surprise me to learn that some baby middle schoolers were indeed conceived that night, from the way some of those kids were dancing. We moms received many compliments regarding the food, many saying it was the most 'unique' and 'tasty' wedding reception buffet they'd ever attended. No one got sick and no one sued, a successful time all around. So far the marriage has also been successful.

What do you get when you cross a Swede and a Korean? A Korwede. Baby Henry was born two years and two months after the ceremony, a kid hankering after Swedish meatballs and bulgogi. Throw in some hot dogs, cheerios, mac 'n' cheese and he's in Korwedian-American heaven.

F

Barbara Grengs
St Paul, Minnesota, USA

Gifts and Gift Lists

The idea of wedding gifts was a good one in the past when most couples were starting out in a home of their own for the first time and needed to have it equipped with everything from bed linen to furniture. Nowadays, however, many couples have already been living together for some time and have established their home. Even if they have been living as 'singles', in the run-up to moving in together they are probably wondering how on earth to fit both his and her belongings into the one place.

These days there is no obligation to expect traditional wedding gifts and instead you can ask guests to contribute to the cost of, say, your honeymoon, or a conservatory for your house, or even a new car. Don't be shy; wedding guests are only too pleased to be guided as to what you need. There are companies that will organise this for you and all you need to do is provide the address so guests can participate. To find these, key **wedding lists** into Google or another search engine, or look up the Wedding Guide in your local *Yellow Pages*.

Second and subsequent marriages

Some people consider it slightly 'bad form' for people getting married for the second time to expect anything other than token gifts. Whether this is justifiable or not rather depends on the circumstances. If a significant number of your guests will have attended your first wedding, or your partner's, it does seem a bit much to expect them to come up with another substantial gift – especially if you and your intended have been living comfortably together for some time in an established home.

However some second wedding circumstances are not like that at all. You may have a completely different circle of friends from that which surrounded you at your first wedding. You, or the groom, may have emerged from a divorce with very little other than the clothes you were standing up in. You may be about to move into a much bigger house to accommodate the entire new step-family and need a number of traditional wedding gift items to equip it.

G

As for the best way to handle wedding gifts for second and subsequent marriages, let commonsense prevail. If you need things, don't feel inhibited about saying so to your guests. But if you are comfortably established, don't be greedy. In fact if you're very comfortably off you could even ask guests to make a contribution to a charity in lieu of buying a gift, rather as people do with funerals.

Also see section titled Second Marriages.

Girlfriends, Bride's

This worry may not be relevant to you, but it does crop up quite often; to your surprise, one or more of your close girlfriends does not seem to be as ecstatic about your impending nuptials as you are.

Strange though it may seem, some of your close friends might be saddened by the fact that you are getting married. That could be because they would like to get married too, or because it makes them reflect on an unsatisfactory relationship or marriage of their own. Or, it could reflect their sadness at the idea – probably unjustified – that you, as their pal, will no longer be one of the crowd.

How do these girls cope? Often by distancing themselves from you and the wedding, or by not taking it seriously. That can result in a distance between you and one or more friends with whom you used to share everything.

The solution? As always, it's communication.

In all probability, girlfriends who feel upset at the thought of your getting married will not want to admit it. But if they are to get over the problem, they need to bring it out into the open. Here's where you come in; you can approach the subject over a coffee or a glass of wine and perhaps mention how you felt upset when one of your other friends got married in the past. The fact that you have been there too (or are pretending to have been there) will make your unhappy friends realise that it's quite a normal thing to feel that way. That way they can open up and talk to you about it, so greatly reducing its pain.

Obviously it helps if you can involve your girlfriends as much as possible in the planning of your wedding and in the day itself. This makes them feel needed and feel part of your happiness, rather than merely being spectators. If there are too many for all to be bridesmaids you can ask one to do a reading during the ceremony; ask another to sing a song or play something on the piano or guitar; ask another to oversee floral decorations or wedding favours; and so on.

And another tip; talk about the future with them. There *is* life beyond the wedding, you know! When you're the bride it's very easy to place all your focus on the wedding day and appear to have stopped thinking about anything beyond getting away for the honeymoon. In the case of girlfriends who fear they'll lose your company in the future, this only adds fuel to the fire. Make sure you chat to them now and again about events that are coming up *after* the wedding, girlie lunches or nights out, and other events and experiences you would share with them.

Groom

What is it about weddings that makes some grooms develop total allergy syndrome and run for the hills until it's time to go to the ceremony?

A cynical view would be that organising a wedding is far too daunting a prospect for men to cope with, so rather than be shown up by the superior organising skills of women, they avoid as much contact with it as possible!

More realistically, I think it's a case that men aren't as good at dealing with detail as women are. They can see the point of, but can't gain much enjoyment from, all the agonising women do over colour schemes, floral choices, menus, dress designs, etc, etc. We women on the other hand can cheerfully lose ourselves in a snowstorm of colour swatches, brochures, pictures and other material that would drive most men mad.

As weddings are a time when emotions can run at a pretty high voltage, some grooms are concerned that if they do offer opinions they might upset the wrong person. Well, that's their excuse, anyway. And some men ... well, just aren't interested. They want to be married, but are intimidated by the fuss of a wedding.

Now, before we go any further on this topic let's get one thing clear; you need to make a decision on whether the groom should be involved in the wedding plans or not. There may be some circumstances in which the bride, her family and friends are more than delighted to run the whole show without interference from elsewhere. If that's the case, move on to the next topic! If not, and you want the groom to be usefully employed in the wedding process, read on here.

What he can do (and still be macho)

G

Most of the wedding etiquette books and websites will give you chapter and verse on the groom's duties on the actual day of the wedding. However there are a number of tasks he can take care of before the day without being obliged to try on different colours of chiffon or select from 87 different designs of table decoration.

Take a cue from the groom's natural capabilities:

- Is he an accountant, finance executive, budget controller? Get him to be in charge of the wedding spend and manage the invoices/payments.

- Is he a project manager or co-ordinator? Ask him to oversee and manage the suppliers working together to create your reception (caterers, florists, entertainers, etc).

- Is he good at decorating, carpentry and/or DIY? Get him to organise a crew to erect decorations – balloons, floral displays, etc – at the wedding venue.

- Does he like food and wine? Put him in charge of selecting the menu and wines for the reception – or even get him to create a new cocktail or wine-based drink specially for the event.

- Is he knowledgeable about cars and transport? Ask him to research the best deals on wedding cars and negotiate with the final supplier.

- Is he a keen photographer? Set him to work researching wedding photography services and deciding on the right one to do your wedding.

Groom's Clothes

One thing the groom has to do whether he likes it or not is to decide what he, the best man and the other male attendants are going to wear, and then to organise those outfits.

If he is going to hire clothes for all the guys – especially if your wedding is during the high season – he must do this in plenty of time if he wants to be sure of getting the right styles and sizes.

If he and the other male participants are to buy their clothes, once again this should be done in plenty of time to ensure the right fit and design. If they don't want to go to the expense of buying entire outfits, they can create an attractive overall look in plain suits (hired or their own) with colour co-ordinated shirts, ties and buttonholes.

And it's helpful if the groom consults with the bride about what the boys should wear!

Guests

Compiling the guest list often is one of the most sensitive elements of organising a wedding. If only it were as simple as just writing down the names of the people you would like to share the day with!

The influencing factors here are as follows, in probable order of importance:

- budget (overall)
- who's paying how much of that budget
- politics and social obligations
- family/cultural/religious traditions.

Budget

How many people you invite to your wedding depends greatly on how many you can afford to accommodate in terms of booze, food and space at the reception. But don't forget, you have a choice of options; you don't necessarily have to have a lavish three course banquet if it means you can't afford to invite some people who really matter to you. A finger buffet or drinks and canapés can be just as elegant and as festive at a far lower cost per head, so you can afford to invite rather more guests. With this option you can also get a greater number of guests into the same space, which helps save even more on the per head cost.

Also see section titled Finances and Budgeting: ways of saving.

Who's paying how much of that budget

This is where tempers can get a little frayed, especially if the wedding is being paid for in the old-fashioned way – i.e. largely by the bride's parents. I remember seething with resentment at my first wedding many years ago when I realised there were some guests there I didn't even know – they were friends of my parents. However as the groom and I were extremely short of money at the time we didn't have a lot of choice.

Nowadays the cost is usually spread far more evenly across all the key parties, so there is much less room for unfair allocation of invitations. Precisely how you carve those up is very much a matter of individual preference, but a useful rule of thumb is one third to the bride's family and friends, one third to the groom's family and friends, and one third to the bride's and groom's own friends. Often you'll find there is a lot of crossover among these lists which allows for more flexibility all round.

G

Politics and social obligations

This category can consist of almost anyone who you feel 'should' be invited without actually deserving the label of being a 'wanted guest'. It includes far-flung, distant relatives you haven't seen for 20 years, a godmother who stopped sending you birthday cards when you were 5 years old, your Dad's boss and his wife, and then all the people whose weddings or whose children's weddings you and your parents have been invited to in the past. In my view these people should be last on the list of priorities, but there may be sound political reasons why they need to be invited. Give and take is needed here, as well as – as always – clear communication between you and the two families.

Family/cultural/religious traditions

Although family traditions are usually easier to negotiate, cultural and religious traditions regarding who has to be invited to a wedding are often non-negotiable without causing World War Three to break out. Couples wishing to avoid going along with such traditions should really consider having a very small, secular wedding – perhaps a destination wedding – rather than try to cope with ill feelings about having to have the traditional variety, and/or paying a fortune for it. They can then be free to celebrate their marriage after the fact, with whoever they please.

Partners too?

You can't really avoid inviting husbands, wives or live-in partners, but do you invite single guests to bring a date? A lot depends on how many guests you can accommodate, both physically and financially. If you don't want single guests to bring someone, in theory all you have to do is just put the single person's name on the invitation without the added 'and partner'. However some people can be bullet-proof and ask if they can bring someone, anyway. See below.

G

Unwanted/uninvited guests

When you get one of those phone calls asking if the person concerned can bring a friend, don't be intimidated into saying yes if you don't want to. There are ways around it.

If you're having a dance after the dinner, you could point out to the person that there is no space for extra people for the meal, but his/her partner is welcome to join you for the dancing afterwards.

If you can't or don't want the partner there at all, say you're sorry, but you're restricted on numbers – however why don't the four of you go for a drink or a meal after the wedding some time, as you'd love to meet the friend concerned – another time.

Work colleagues

This can be a tricky one too. You can't necessarily afford to invite everyone you work with, but if you only invite a few will the others be offended? Once again I think you should play the money card here and say you'd love to invite everyone but simply can't afford to, so why don't we have a party or drinks after work to celebrate that way?

If you do invite work colleagues it makes sense to invite all those with whom you work closely. This strays into the area of politics (see above), but the last thing you want to do is offend someone who sits opposite or next to you for eight hours a day five days a week.

If you're in sales, and/or are self-employed, you may wonder what to do about your best clients or customers. You have to use your commonsense here; do you really want them to see you and your personal life in all its glory at the wedding? Are they the sort of people who would also be personal friends?

If you have any doubts about those two points then don't invite them. If they feel they don't fit in with the rest of your crowd and don't know anyone else, they won't enjoy the wedding very much. At the same time you will feel a little awkward about them being there. If you get the impression that they would like to celebrate with you, however, organise a separate meal, party or drinks for your customers or clients and key staff, if appropriate, as well as your intended, of course!

Make sure your invitations are clear

When you send out the invitations make sure the wording is clear and that guests know exactly when and where they should turn up. If you want the party to end at a specific time, make that clear too. This avoids misunderstandings and guests being mislaid! It's especially important to make the places and timings clear when your guest list includes friends from other cultures and nationalities, as their expectations of how a wedding works might be different from yours – see Jonathan's contribution below.

Don't forget to RSVP

A Hindu friend was asked to an English (very) wedding breakfast and just turned up to the occasion after the marriage ceremony. He was mortified when he discovered that there was no place set for him, but the hosts did manage to squeeze him in. By contrast at an Indian wedding guests are supposed to come and turn up as they feel and there are never any difficulties in providing a few extra places. The answer is to RSVP and keep to your promise!

Jonathan Heywood, UK

Hairstyles

See section titled Bride's Dress, Hair and Make-Up.

Honeymoons

Honeymoons perhaps aren't in my remit as they're not strictly part of weddings, but as they are so closely associated here are my thoughts on what, if any, worries could arise and how to help ensure they don't.

Firstly, never fall into the trap of leaving the arrangements for your honeymoon too late. Even if you're only going to a country house hotel 20 miles away for a couple of nights, you want to be sure you get the booking you want and preferably, the bridal suite! Also you may find that by booking well in advance you can negotiate a better price.

Don't overplan your honeymoon

When you're contemplating your honeymoon while relaxed, rested and refreshed months before the wedding, it's all too easy to think in terms of planning vigorous sight-seeing, strenuous tours, minimalist back-packing, energetic sports or other lively activities. What you must remember is that even if you are both 25-year-old fitness fanatics, you are going to be tired after all the exertions and stress of your wedding, and if your honeymoon journey is quite long you'll be tired because of that too. So even if you do want to spend most of the time playing tennis or climbing mountains, be kind to yourselves – plan in a few days of rest and relaxation first.

Remember to make arrangements for your wedding night

The old image of bride and groom driving off from the wedding reception to their honeymoon venue in a smart car dangling tin cans from the back bumper has become something of an urban legend. After your wedding, probably the last thing in the world you'll want to do is get in a car and drive somewhere – not to mention the undesirability of that in the light of drink–drive laws.

If you are going abroad or some distance away for your honeymoon it's probably best either to book yourselves a room at the reception venue, or at least nearby, so you can tumble into bed after the reception and have a good rest. Do yourselves a favour – save the travelling for later.

H

Don't push yourselves to make an early start next day

Even though it might be cheaper to book an early ferry or flight the day after your wedding, be kind to yourselves and allow enough time for a leisurely start and rush-free journey to the airport or other point of departure. You may have had a good night's sleep, but you will still feel tired.

Remember to sort out passports and other travel documents

This may sound ridiculous, but it is something that easily can be overlooked in the flurry of preparations for a wedding: make sure your passports are up to date, and do that in plenty of time. Passport renewal can take a while and you don't want to be worrying about that while organising everything else. Also ensure that you have your travel documents safely ensconced in the care of someone you trust, so they are readily to hand after the wedding.

Accommodation: twin beds?

Chances are you would probably prefer to share a double bed on your honeymoon ... however many hotels, cruise ships and other accommodations tend to offer more in the way of twin-bedded accommodation. When booking your honeymoon make sure that your room has a double, not twin-bedded option. If necessary, tell them why you want that.

Tell them you're on honeymoon

Some people shrink away from the extra attention they might get as honeymooners, but that's not necessarily a good idea. Normally if you book standard accommodations in an hotel the fact that you're honeymooners won't raise the price, but in fact quite the opposite – the hotel is likely to throw in some free goodies which probably are well worth having.

Pack for your honeymoon in plenty of time

Unless you're intending to leave a few days' gap between the wedding and your honeymoon, don't leave shopping and packing for the trip until the last minute. You'll have enough on your plate in the immediate run-up to the wedding without worrying whether that new bikini will fit or the rock-climbing caribiners are of the right size.

Also see sections titled Destination Weddings, and Finances and Budgeting.

H

Horse-Drawn Vehicles

I know lots of people these days fancy the idea of being driven to the ceremony and to the reception in a beautiful horse-drawn carriage, or even in a small cart pulled by a pony. I know there are numerous companies that specialise in supplying horse-drawn vehicles for weddings and make a good living out of it.

I also know horses and ponies very well, having ridden them most of my life and known many people who are into carriage driving.

If this is something you are contemplating, I hate to be a killjoy, but think carefully. Unless it's an experienced wedding carriage puller, even the most placid and laid-back horse or pony is unlikely to be comfortable with crowds of people waving and shouting excitedly. And even those experienced carriage pullers can be spooked by a car backfiring or other sudden, loud noise.

You might think that a couple of dear old cart horses couldn't possibly be anything other than sweetness and light as they pull you to your dream wedding. But if you have ever seen a couple of 19 hand Shires spook at full gallop (I have, and it's terrifying) you may prefer to consider a more mechanical option.

If after all my wet-blanket ravings you still want to go the horse-drawn route, here's my advice.

Horse-drawn wedding vehicle companies

There are many of these around and you'll find them in your local *Yellow Pages* or online via Google or other search engine.

Having got to know the people and horses involved in quite a successful such company local to me, I have to say, check carefully and get some personal recommendations first. The company I got to know used young, inexperienced horses and equally young (therefore cheap) and inexperienced drivers. In the main they got away with it when they had wedding groups on board, but they did have some dreadful accidents when loading and unloading horses and vehicles.

Ask the company for references and also visit their yard and ask to meet their horses. If the horses look calm, clean and in good health you're probably OK. Beware horses that seem shy, skittish, sweated up, underweight, or with scars on their heads and other harness areas of their bodies (mainly the neck, shoulders and back).

H

Private horse-drawn vehicles

Ironically this may be the better option, especially if you know the horse's owner well and trust him or her and his/her judgment. A privately owned horse is likely to be more of a docile pet than one owned by a carriage yard and is also likely to have a better relationship with its owner/driver.

Almost certainly the owner will want to rehearse the journey with the horse (beware if s/he doesn't) so it doesn't encounter any surprises on the day. You might enjoy going along for the ride, if you have time, to make sure you don't have any previously unknown qualms about horse-drawn transport. Also, assuming the vehicle used for the rehearsal is the same one to be used on the day, you can check out realistically how easy or hard it will be to climb up into and down from the vehicle in your wedding attire.

It's a good idea to warn as many of your bridal party and guests as possible that on the day you will be arriving and departing via real, live horsepower, and tell them not to do anything that could cause a fright.

Inter-Faith Weddings

People's experiences with inter-faith weddings range from the utterly awful to the delightful. Much depends on how tolerant and mature the two families are, and how seriously they observe their own religious values and traditions.

The prospect of an inter-faith wedding can be very daunting, but remember there are ways of handling it that can result in a wedding that is meaningful for you and that pleases both religious factions involved.

Give it time

Many people say that time is a great healer and this is certainly the case here. Should the announcement of your engagement cause a stir with one or both families for religious reasons, remember that as time progresses everyone will get used to the idea. For that reason, amongst others, it's sensible to have quite a long engagement.

Spend as much time as you can with each family and learn all you can about the other religion. Be honest with them about your concerns and encourage them to be honest with you. Some families will see your choosing to marry out of the faith as a rejection of the values they hold dear, and will be deeply hurt. Over time you can compensate for this by showing that you are not turning your back on your own religion and that the values it – and your family – have taught you will never be forgotten.

This period will also allow for what may amount to a more complex religious build-up to the wedding than would be the case otherwise. One partner may decide to convert to the other's religion, which can take quite a long time. And whatever religious option you choose, it will take time to find the right solution, the right officiants, and the right venues.

What if the family refuses to accept it?

If after a reasonable length of time and effort on your part to communicate with and listen to your family's concerns they still won't accept your decision to marry out of their faith, you may just have to go ahead and do it without them. It will be very painful for you and probably very painful for them, but in the end it is your life and provided you are convinced you're making the right decision, that should take priority.

As time goes on and your family can see for themselves that you're happy and settled, they may well relent; after all your happiness matters greatly to them, no matter what their religious convictions. Also, you may find that barriers come down when there is a grandchild in the offing.

What is important is that you don't cut yourself off from your family. Keep the door open. If they have taken a firm stand against your marriage they probably will find it quite hard to eat humble pie and contact you again, so make it as easy as possible for them. Even if you feel angry with them – as well you might, to begin with at least – remember that they are still your family and that there's a good chance of reconciliation some day in the future.

What are the options?

Couples from two different religious backgrounds basically have a choice of five options:

1. *One partner converts to the other's religion.*

2. *You have two ceremonies (or blessings following a civil marriage), one within each religion.*

3. *You have a ceremony that combines the two religions.*

4. *You create a non-denominational ceremony.*

5. *You marry in a register office and do not have a religious wedding at all.*

Conversion

This is not something I can advise on and strictly speaking isn't within the remit of this book! Obviously the choice of whether to do it, and if so who does what, is entirely a matter for discussion and agreement between you two and your families. You must also seek the advice of your own religious leaders before you make the final decision. Whatever you do, though, make sure you keep your families informed of what you're doing, and be as understanding and caring as possible. Misunderstandings of this kind cause a great deal of hurt – see Lynn's contribution, below.

Jewish/Christian

Although I married out of the Jewish faith both our daughters were raised within it, with both having bat mitzvahs and generally observing the religion. When one of my daughters went to university, however, she converted to Christianity and became quite seriously involved with it. When she became engaged to another Christian she insisted that they be married in a Church of England ceremony.

Although the vicar was very understanding of the fact that my daughter's family are all Jewish and agreed to temper the service to make it as secular as possible, all the same some of our family refused to come to the service.

This was made all the worse for the fact that my daughter insisted on holding the wedding on a Friday afternoon, which of course meant that the more religious members of our family were not able to join us for the evening celebrations as Friday night to Saturday night is the Jewish Sabbath.

In the circumstances it really would have been better if they had had a civil wedding, not on a Friday or Saturday, so that there wouldn't have been any of the ill feeling that inevitably crept in. I know it was my daughter's day and everything, but even as the bride you can't totally ignore your family's faith and beliefs. They could have followed on with religious blessings if they wanted to.

Lynn, UK

Two ceremonies

Provided that both religions will allow this, it strikes me as a very good solution to the dilemma. You will need to check out the legal implications here. If one of the two ceremonies includes the registry bit that's required in the UK that's fine; alternatively you can have a civil wedding first with blessing ceremonies within each religion afterwards, or arrange to have a registrar present at one of the two ceremonies.

Combination ceremony

This is another good idea provided you can make it work! Within different sectors of the same religion, e.g. Roman Catholicism and Anglican Christians, Liberal and Orthodox Judaism, etc, it shouldn't be too difficult to organise a ceremony that is acceptable to all parties; see Nick Terry's contribution below.

RC rules

I come from a strong Roman Catholic background and married a girl who was Church of Wales. She was advised by her vicar that in the Roman Catholic Church's eye we would not be properly married. This of course totally ignored the concept of law, etc!

My Mum, a heavy Roman Catholic, wasn't comfortable with me marrying out of the faith.

The solution? We got my Mum's priest to help officiate at the wedding. The result? Everyone was happy!

Nick Terry
Top Banana
www.top-b.com
UK

Where things might get a bit more complex is when there is a greater difference between the two religions. This need not be a problem, however. As usual, it's a matter of communication! Talk to your religious leaders about your desire to blend the two religions into one ceremony. It could well be that they take a more flexible view of this than you would have imagined.

A non-denominational ceremony

There are officiants – some ordained ministers – who will put together a non-denominational ceremony for your wedding. This will assume only that you both believe in a 'higher being', without going into the specifics of a particular religious viewpoint.

You will have to check carefully what the current legislation is regarding such weddings and, if necessary, have a register office marriage in addition. To find these people in the UK key **interfaith ministers** into Google UK or other UK search engine.

For more information on inter-faith weddings, key **interfaith weddings** into Google or other search engine.

Invitations

See sections titled Guests, and Second Marriages.

Marquees

Marquees are a wonderful invention – they provide relatively instant large scale accommodation that transforms a house into a vast wedding venue (assuming the garden's big enough) and leaves hardly a trace behind afterwards other than a few holes in the lawn where the pegs were dug in. They're not cheap to hire, but in some circumstances save quite a lot on venue hire and in any case can give you the chance to have your wedding reception at home, despite the fact that 200 guests would have to be stacked horizontally were they to be entertained in the house itself.

As in so many other instances if you are going to hire a marquee yourself, try if you can to get personal recommendations of local companies. And don't try to economise here. Boy Scout marquees – a.k.a large tents – can be very cheap, but also can be rather dirty and full of holes.

Proper marquees designed for functions come with all the necessary accessories, including heating should that be needed. However be warned here: often marquees are heated by giant hot air blowers which, though efficient, tend to be noisy. That means that they will need to be turned off during the speeches, even if you use microphones.

If your wedding is taking place in cooler months you might find that your guests get pretty chilly, especially if dad or Uncle Bernard go on at length about your first bicycle and how you learned to ride it, or the best man gets carried away telling jokes. It may be worth your while talking to the marquee supplier to see whether a quieter form of heating can be used, or alternatively you may need to keep the speeches pretty short.

Mothers

A girl's relationship with her mother is hardly ever uncomplicated. Often it is a mixture of intense love and closeness with a hidden streak of competitiveness or even rivalry. Most of us muddle along if things get tense between us and our mothers, and provided everyone behaves in a mature, adult way any issues can be resolved.

When it comes to a daughter's wedding, though, all this calm, good sense can get thrown out of the window, especially when it's the first child or first daughter to marry.

Why your relationship changes

No matter how modern your mother is and how well attuned she is to gender equality, there is no doubt that your relationship with her will change once you get engaged. The politically correct brigade probably will want to shout at me here, but in my view it will take more than a few generations to breed out the long-standing notions we women have been brought up to believe about the status of marriage. Being a married woman is different to being a single woman whether in a mere titular way, or – as is the case in many more traditional cultures – in quite a substantial way where her standing in her community is concerned.

This then shifts the balance of the mother–daughter relationship from one of parent–child to one of equality. Your mother may kid herself that you're still her little girl until you're a single woman in your 30s or 40s, but once she knows you're headed up that aisle she is obliged to remove her head from the sand and recognise you as a fellow adult. Whether she likes it or not she has been moved up through another rite of passage in her life; she is a stage closer to old age. That can be quite depressing for her, especially if she is menopausal at the same time.

In a way, she is grieving for two losses; you in your role as the single daughter, and her own youth.

So no matter how subtle, there will be a change in your relationship with your mother. You may not be looking for it and she may well try to conceal it, but it can emerge in a number of different ways as preparations for the wedding get going. She might display a number of different behaviours you find surprising; she may become argumentative, bossy, distant, critical, sarcastic and even jealous.

How to handle her

As is the case in so many other areas of life, knowing what the real problem is can get you halfway towards solving it. Once you know that your mother is probably feeling quite sad, it will help you to see how she might be channelling that sadness into strange behaviour. What you need to do is to try not to react to her behaviour, but to be as caring and loving as you can be so she feels supported. Don't be angry with her; much as her strange behaviour may be awkward for you, always remember that the problem lies with her, not with you.

It's also very important to talk with your mother as much as you can, and to be totally honest about how you feel. People always associate weddings with radiant happiness, but actually they are also a time when you say goodbye to certain elements of your life, which can be sad for you too. If you talk openly about any little regrets you may have at the thought of moving on to the next stage of your life, your mother may feel more comfortable about admitting her own feelings of regret – perhaps not to you, but at least to herself. Candid discussion about how you both feel, provided that it doesn't begin opening up old wounds, is a far healthier alternative than brushing the sad elements of the wedding under the carpet.

M

The overbearing types

Many mothers are excellent organisers and are a godsend for a busy bride who hasn't got time to see to every last detail. However there are many mothers who will take this role too far, and become somewhat overbearing and bossy.

Even if your wedding is of the old-fashioned variety where the bride's parents are paying for most of it, there is still a lot you can do to sidestep conflicts with your mother despite her running the whole project like a military boot camp.

Whatever you do, avoid direct confrontations. These nearly always lead to more trouble, including the emergence of recriminations and old disagreements crawling out of the woodwork. By far the better policy is to create diversions, either practical or psychological. For example, if you want to commission and order the floral arrangements yourself, but your mother wants to be involved in it too, say that you want her to devote that portion of her time to something 'far more important', i.e. another element of the wedding you're not so concerned about.

One of your mother's greatest fears at this pivotal time of her life is of being redundant. Any suggestion that she is not wanted in any area of wedding preparations will reinforce this fear and may make her moody or aggressive, or create other unfortunate reactions. By diverting her away from something while involving her further in another area, you are achieving more or less what you want without hurting her feelings.

Mothers-in-Law

What would joke writers and stand-up comedians do without mothers-in-law?

M

My mother-in-law called today ...
I knew it was her. When she knocked on the front door all the mice threw themselves into the traps.

A woman walked out of a smart restaurant wearing an elegant real fur coat. She was approached by another woman who asked disapprovingly, 'And what poor creature had to die so you could wear that?'
'My mother-in-law,' smiled the first woman.

My mother-in-law and I were happy for 20 years. Then we met each other.

Q: What are the two worst things about your mother-in-law?
A: Her faces.

And so it goes on. Why is the poor old mother-in-law such a popular source of humour? Because your relationship with her can be one of the most challenging relationships you've ever had.

On the other hand, of course, many women have great relationships with their mothers-in-law. And that's amazing when you consider the emotional issues that often exist between them.

What are her problems?

Just as fathers can be possessive about their daughters and feel grief at having to hand their little girls over to other men (see section titled Fathers), mothers can be and often are very possessive about their sons.

Even though she might be quite happy and relaxed about your relationship with her son while you were just going out or even living together, the fact that you are now getting married and that there is to be another Mrs Whoever, changes the picture. Now she has to face the fact that her son is replacing her as the number one woman in his life – with you.

No matter how philosophical a woman is, I think this is hard for her to accept. I know that when my son gets married I will feel, deep down, a sense of desertion and grief, no matter how much I like my new daughter-in-law. Just as is the case with your own mother, your wedding is a rite of passage for everyone else in your close family, mother-in-law included. The big difference between your mother and your mother-in-law is that the latter lady didn't give birth to you and doesn't love you the way your own mother does, although of course she may come to do so in time. So any sensation of jealousy, rivalry, competition, etc will not be cushioned by any familial love or loyalty.

Your mother-in-law may well have had a very close relationship with your fiancé, perhaps looking after his domestic needs and generally spoiling him. In her eyes this will be a very hard act for you to follow, especially if you, like most rational people, think that the 'domesticated little woman' role sucks and that your husband-to-be can damned well iron his own shirts. Worse still, your mother-in-law may try to extend her running of her son's domestic life into your life together. While it may be handy to have someone to help with the domestics, do you really want your mother-in-law to run your life?

Being good enough

Another mother-in-law issue is that no girl would ever be good enough for what she had in mind for her darling boy. This standpoint is a useful excuse to cover up jealousy, because whatever you are and whatever you do, it won't be good enough to meet her constantly shifting standards.

Well, that's all the bad news. What can be done to reduce the negative issues and get into a better relationship with her?

Your fiancé's role

Let's face it, if your fiancé has always been a bit of a mummy's boy you're in for an uphill struggle, but it's a struggle you must get through if there is to be a peaceful relationship with her once you're married. If things are tricky between you and your future mother-in-law, the first thing to do is to get your fiancé to sit her down privately, point out that he is not a little boy any longer, and that it's very important to him that you and she get along as well as possible.

He must also make the point that if push comes to shove, he will side with you, not her. That's something that he will have to stick to, as well, no matter how much pressure his mother might put on him to do otherwise.

He may well dread the idea of confronting his mother in this way and she may well shout and squirm to begin with. However provided that he stands his ground in a kind but firm way, in time she will have to accept it. In fact she will probably come to respect both her son and you more, for the fact that the issue has been faced and dealt with openly.

Your role

I think it's very important for you, as the bride, to develop your own relationship with your future mother-in-law, independently of your fiancé and other family members.

To begin with, you owe it to both her and yourself to devote quite a lot of time and energy to this relationship. Whatever you may think of her she is still your fiancé's mother, and as such is a very important part of your lives.

In addition, for all you know she may be more nervous about her new relationship with you than you think, and could feel unsure how to handle it.

Try to organise a lunch or shopping trip with just you and her, so you can get to know each other as people rather than in your respective family roles. You and she might both be pleasantly surprised at how well you get along when there's no one else around to divert your attention from each other.

If she wants to be involved in helping organise your wedding, try to accommodate her wish and make her feel not only needed, but admired for her capabilities. It's very easy for the groom's family to feel a little left out of things when a wedding is being planned because most of the organisation is normally driven by the bride, and by extension her family and her friends. If mother-in-law should, by any chance, become a bit too pushy, try diverting her energy into one specific channel in a tactful way (also see section titled Mothers).

Mothers' Outfits

What the bride's and bridegroom's mothers wear is becoming almost as important as what the bride wears. Without trying too hard it can turn into a major political issue, illustrated here by a joke about rehearsal dinners (see section titled Rehearsals and Rehearsal Dinners).

The wedding day was nearly there.

Everything was ready. Nothing could dilute Claudia's excitement – not even her parents' bitter divorce.

Her mother Marian finally found the perfect outfit to wear and would be the best-dressed mother of the bride of all time.

A week later Claudia was horrified to learn her young stepmother, Eleanor, had bought the same dress. Claudia asked Eleanor to change the dress for something else, but Eleanor said, 'No way! I'll look amazing in it!'

Claudia told her mother, who sincerely replied, 'Never mind darling. I'll get another dress. For Heaven's sake – it's your day, not hers.'

Two weeks later Marian finally had acquired another dress. Afterwards, over lunch, Claudia asked her mother, 'What are you going to do with the first dress? Maybe you should take it back to the shop. You're not likely to wear it anywhere else.'

M

Marian grinned and replied, 'Of course I will, darling! I'll wear it to the rehearsal dinner!'

Strictly speaking mothers' outfits shouldn't be the bride's problem, but in some cases they do stray into that territory. Many companies selling brides' dresses also stock outfits for mothers of the bride/groom, and these can be useful sources, as well as providing a convenient solution.

However don't allow yourself to be drawn into a political battle over mothers' outfits. If they want to make that a platform for political or other one-upmanship, let them – it's not your problem. Thankfully, although some mothers may start out with an adversarial attitude to what they will wear, usually in the end they decide to be sensible and wear what suits them, but doesn't upstage you – or each other.

Music

See section titled Entertainment.

Names

Do you have to change to your husband's name after you're married?

The short answer is no.

The legalities of names are quite complex in the UK although, in theory at least, you're entitled to call yourself whatever you like provided you follow the procedures. I asked UK solicitor Sue McGaughran to give us chapter and verse on this topic, so here it is,

---

Changing your name: advice from UK solicitor Sue McGaughran

There are various circumstances in which a person may want to change their name. You can change your name at any time, but one of the most common ones is when you get married. However, some couples like to change names earlier than marriage, when they are just thinking about getting married or when they move in together, for example, and are buying a house.

You don't actually need a 'legal' reason to change your name – you can change it just because you want to be known by another name. In this section we will be dealing with persons 18 and over who wish to change their names. Other criteria and conditions apply for those who are younger and parents who wish to change their child's names.

There are few restrictions on what a person can call themselves, provided they:

- use at least one surname and one forename and
- the name doesn't use numbers or punctuations (except a hyphen to link names)
- is not vulgar, blasphemous or otherwise offensive
- is not impossible to pronounce and
- will not result in passing off, for deceit or fraud, or to make anyone believe you hold a title that you don't actually have (e.g. Baron, Colonel, etc).

After those rules pretty well anything goes. There are several people called Elvis Presley alive and well and living in the UK.

How can I change my name?

On a birth certificate

There currently are only several, very limited, circumstances when you can actually get your name changed on your birth certificate. These include changing a child's surname when the child's parents were not married at the time of the child's birth and when a person has changed gender and can obtain a Gender Recognition Certificate. As you'd expect, various criteria need to be met.

On marriage

N

When a couple get married, whilst it is common for a woman to change her surname to use her husband's surname, it is not compulsory. For example, Rachel Smith marries Robert Brown. Rachel can simply call herself Rachel Brown and can send a copy of her marriage certificate to the relevant government bodies (passport, etc) and bank, etc as proof of her new name. Her name will be changed to reflect her new married surname.

However, it is also legal for the woman to retain her own name. In our example, if Rachel wants to acknowledge she is now married, but prefers to use her own surname, she can call herself Mrs Rachel Smith. In these circumstances Rachel may want to make a Statutory Declaration to reflect her new status, from Miss to Mrs, but bearing in mind she is just changing her title and not her name this is not really necessary. Most documents just reflect her name (such as driving licence) and not her title. For documents that do reflect her title, such as her cheque book, simply writing to the bank, explaining the situation and enclosing a copy of her marriage certificate should be enough in these circumstances.

Double barrelled. Increasingly, couples are choosing to take both surnames and make them double-barrelled. In our example of Rachel this may be, for example,

Brown-Smith. The couple can choose any order they like for the surnames and both can use the 'new name'.

Meshing surnames. Likewise, lots of couples are choosing to take both surnames and make a completely new surname using them. In our example of Rachel this may be, for example Smithbrown. Again, the choice is completely their own.

In both these examples it is easy for the man to make a Statutory Declaration (see below) or Deed Poll (see below) that he will send to the relevant bodies (see Who do I need to tell? below) so that he can ensure that all his documents reflect his new name. There are two ways of approaching this, once the couple have decided on the new name. Either in our example,

- Robert takes the new name first by either Statutory Declaration or Deed Poll (as below) before the couple marry. This means when they marry Rachel can take her husband's name and there is no need for her to make a Statutory Declaration or Deed Poll. This is the most cost-effective and efficient way.

- Both Robert and Rachel change their names by either Statutory Declaration or Deed Poll (as below) after the marriage. They can actually do this on their wedding day, just after getting married, if they prefer.

Although we have discussed changing their surnames on marriage, when they are making the Statutory Declaration or Deed Poll they can also change their forenames, or rearrange the order of forenames, etc.

Civil partnerships

Again, there is no legal requirement for one party to take the other's surname. They have the same options as those who marry of:

i)   changing one person's surname to the other

ii) double barrelling

iii) meshing

iv) both changing their names completely.

Most of those options do require the couple making Statutory Declarations or Deed Polls, as in the examples above for married couples.

However, just as on marriage if one person simply wishes to take the other person's name (for example Anne Jones is entering into a civil partnership with Wendy Gray and the couple want Anne to be called Anne Gray), the Civil Partnership Certificate allows for this. Just as if in our example, when Rachel marries Robert and wishes to become Rachel Brown and uses her marriage certificate to send to the relevant government bodies (see Who do I need to tell?, below) for her name to be changed, Anne does the same with her Civil Partnership Certificate.

Changing a name by Deed Poll at any time

This doesn't change a person's name on their birth certificate and is effectively a legal document that declares that the person wishes to be known by a new name and intends, from the date of the deed, to be known by that name. It is signed by the person who wishes to change their name in front of a witness. Lawyers can draw this up for you and packs are available if you wish to do the work yourself.

Changing a name by Statutory Declaration at any time

Again, this doesn't change a person's name on their birth certificate. It is a legal document that declares that the person wishes to be known by a new name and intends, from the date of the declaration, to be known by that name. It is signed by the person who wishes to change their name in front of a Commissioner (e.g. any qualified solicitor) who 'witnesses it'.

Why use a Deed Poll or a Statutory Declaration?

Both these documents are documentary evidence of your new name. There is no compulsory central register of either of these documents. It is possible to get a Deed Poll 'enrolled' – this is a public record and means the Deed is also published (along with the person's address, etc) in the *London* (or *Belfast*) *Gazette*. However this is expensive, takes time and is not usually necessary.

In theory there is no reason why you can't just decide to change your name and write to people to let them know your new name. However, because most organisations want some written proof of the change, you will usually find that it will result in a lot of work in completing lots of documents for each organisation you notify, and will take longer than making a Deed Poll or a Statutory Declaration at the start. Some organisations (e.g. some banks, etc) won't accept a letter and want a Deed Poll or a Statutory Declaration anyway and will send you one to complete. In addition you may be asked to produce a letter from a 'responsible person' (e.g. your GP) to show that you have been using the new name. You shouldn't have to do this if you have a properly completed Deed Poll or a Statutory Declaration.

N

What is the difference between a Deed Poll and a Statutory Declaration?

There is no real difference in everyday matters between changing your name by a Deed Poll to changing your name by Statutory Declaration, save that the Statutory Declaration is sworn before a Commissioner.

How do I let people know that I have changed my name?

With both documents the person changing their name simply sends it off to the relevant bodies (see Who do I need to tell?, below). Those documents will then be changed to reflect the new name.

Who do I need to tell about my change of name?

In both the Deed Poll and the Statutory Declaration a person confirms that they are abandoning their old name and will be using their new name. This means that you should tell everybody – here are a few suggestions:

✓ HMRC (Inland Revenue for tax purposes)

✓ Passport Agency (to get a new passport in the new name)

✓ DVLA (to get a new driving licence in the new name)

✓ Employer, college, etc

✓ GP, dentist and anyone else providing medical treatment

✓ Bank, building society, credit cards, savings, loans, etc

✓ Utility organisations – water, gas, electric, telephone, etc

✓ Local Authority (register of Electors, Council Tax)

✓ Landlord/mortgage company

✓ HM Land Registry (so the house deeds (land or charge certificate) show the new name)

✓ Insurances – house, life, health, etc

✓ Clubs, subscriptions, etc.

N

Legalisation

Couples getting married abroad may find that their documents such as birth certificates and Deed Polls or Statutory Declarations need to be 'legalised'. This is simply a process whereby the UK government confirm that the signature, seal or stamp appearing on the document is genuine.

This process is dealt with by the Legalisation Office at the Foreign and Commonwealth office at Old Admiralty Building, The Mall, London SW1A 2LG by post or by personal attendance.

Sue McGaughran
Solicitor, Lime One Ltd
www.limeone.co.uk

Please note Sue's advice is up to date as at November 2006. Laws and circumstances regarding names may change over time, so check the current position with Sue, or with your own legal advisers.

Nerves and Stress

Nerves and stress have been given bad names by the media and are commonly seen as public enemy number one when it comes to people's enjoyment and fulfilment. What people forget is that a reasonable amount of nervousness, and a good squirt of stress hormones pumping around your body, help prepare you for any challenging activity you are about to undertake.

Remember the old 'fight or flight' gag? Well, although your wedding may not have many similarities with the approach of a hungry lion, no one has got around to informing our hormonal system about it yet. Consequently our reaction to the impending stress of the wedding is, chemically at least, just the same as it would be on sight of that hungry lion: a surge of stress hormones.

And why do we have this surge of stress hormones? To get us right up on our toes so we think, act and move as effectively as possible … whether it is either to kill or run away from the lion (fight or flight) or walk down that aisle and get up to make that wedding speech.

Mind you, in the days when we lived in caves and had serious problems with four-legged predators, the stress hormones released on an impromptu encounter with a lion would be more than used up by our efforts to strangle the beast or run like hell in the opposite direction.

Much as pre-wedding worries can seem as frightening as a peckish lion the reality is that in the run-up to our wedding we don't use up as much of that hormonal energy as we produce. (Don't quote me here, I'm no expert; these are just my own observations. No doubt an endocrinologist would say I'm nuts, but at totally lay level it seems to make sense.) Anyway, the net result is that the left-over stress hormones hang around inside us and create symptoms such as sleeplessness, irritability, headaches, and all manner of other unpleasant effects.

What to do about it

Well, my first piece of advice may seem ridiculous to begin with, but don't worry about it. It's perfectly normal that you should feel nervous and stressed about your wedding. It would be very strange, abnormal, and frankly rather worrying if you *didn't* feel a bit nervous and stressed about your wedding.

To combat the effects of stress on your body you need to start planning for it as soon as possible after you get engaged. Despite there being pressure on you to run around taking on extra duties over and above your work and your domestics, now more than ever it's crucial that you take time out to look after yourself properly.

Eat healthily and make sure you keep exercising in whatever way you normally do. Don't succumb to an increase in smoking, drinking, or use of recreational substances because although those may seem to calm you down and relax you short term, they'll make life more difficult for you over time.

Most important of all, in my opinion, is to look after your sanity. Set some time aside to go out with your girlfriends and forget all about the wedding for a night ... have a romantic dinner with your fiancé at which you both promise not to mention wedding plans ... book yourself in for that facial and massage you've been promising yourself ... take a weekend off to go hiking or mountain biking or pony trekking or sight-seeing ... keep reminding yourself that you and your fiancé have a life, as well as a wedding, to plan.

If you have trouble sleeping, read up on ways to sleep better and then activate those rigorously. Avoid chemical sleep remedies as they nearly all stop working after a few days, and some leave you feeling drowsy the next day. There are several herbal remedies that can help not only with sleep, but also to calm your nerves; the staff at your local health food store will be able to advise you on the best choices. You can also look for such remedies on the internet, but I'm not keen on buying that type of product online as you have no guarantee of quality, unless you buy from well known brands like Holland & Barrett.

N Plan ahead for it

No matter what you do to reduce the effects of stress, you're still likely to be nervous on the day, and all being well some of that nervousness will help keep you on your toes (see above).

However it does make sense to allow in a personalised way for the fact that you will be a bit stressed and nervous.

Think back to a previous occasion when you were nervous and under pressure. How did that nervousness manifest itself? Did it make you clumsy? Did it make you run late and get behind schedule? Did it make you forget things? Did it make you snappy with others?

Analyse carefully how that stress is likely to affect your behaviour on your wedding day and prepare for it, even if it means not operating machines or electrical appliances yourself (clumsy), allowing double the time you think you need for every key activity (running late), writing out a clear 'to do' list for your hair, make-up, getting ready, etc (forgetful) and reminding yourself to think before you shout (snappy!).

Outdoor Weddings

This may seem an obvious one, but even within my own personal experience of attending weddings I know that some organisers are really pushing their luck by choosing to hold the wedding outdoors.

In a region or country where good weather can be virtually guaranteed at certain times of year there is no problem. But whatever happens don't plan on an outdoor wedding anywhere in the world where the weather might spoil the day. And remember, there are months in which it can rain very, very hard even in locations we Europeans consider exotic and tropical – e.g. Africa, south-east Asia, the Caribbean, etc).

Although a contingency plan (i.e. an indoor alternative to switch to at the last minute) is a good idea as an insurance policy in this case, it seldom will be more than second-best.

A safer choice is to pick a location where the main ceremony and formal reception elements are held indoors, but with the option of spilling out on to an adjacent deck, patio or terrace for informal mingling and chatting.

If you're planning to hold your wedding outdoors anywhere but on your own home territory, check up with the local tourist authority for information about their weather and find out when they experience their rainy/hurricane/cyclone/monsoon seasons. Try to plan your wedding at a time when the sun really will shine on you!

Also see the section titled Destination Weddings.

Shoes

This may not seem an important issue, but can make a huge difference to the bride's and other women's comfort. If you're planning to hold your wedding or reception out of doors and will be required to walk on grass or other soft surface, make sure your shoes have heels sufficiently wide that you won't sink. Although killer stilettos or even kitten heels look lovely, you won't think they're lovely if you have to haul your feet out of several centimetres' depth of lawn each time you want to move.

0

Pages

See sections titled Bridesmaids, Flower Girls and Pages and Children.

Parents and Step-Parents

I know there's a lot in this book already about individual parents, but those sections (Fathers; Mothers; Mothers-in-law) focus on the intensely personal issues that can arise. In addition to that there are quite a few further worries associated with parents that aren't so deeply personal, but are still very important to examine – and if we can, put right.

Adoptive vs birth parents

If you and/or your fiancé are adopted and in touch with the birth parents, should they be invited to your wedding?

Obviously this depends very much on the relationships between you and the birth parents, as well as between you and the adoptive parents. When difficulties do arise it tends to be a fear of hurting the adoptive parents' feelings by inviting the birth parents who, despite having done little or nothing towards the raising of the child, seem now to usurp the adoptive parents in the wedding pecking order.

Whatever you decide to do in these circumstances, remember that you are *not* tied to traditions any more; you have alternatives. You do not have to choose whether to have your adoptive father or your birth father walk you down the aisle; you can walk it alone, with the groom, or if you must be given away, by your brother, sister, or best friend.

Lateral thinking is a useful skill not just in business and physics, but also within families. Remember with the whole issue of adoptive parents and birth parents, what counts at the end of the day is what will make *you* happy. If the parents involved get tetchy or offended at the thought of each others' presence, reassure them that you will not place anyone in an embarrassing situation, and that you love them all dearly. Chances are any negative feelings will be the result of insecurity – wondering whether they have been replaced in your affections – so reassurance is critical.

But if you want them all there, have them. It's your day.

Disapproving parents

That can be a tough one. Very tough. But as is the case with so many other things, time and understanding can work wonders.

If one or other of you is disapproved of by one set of parents, the first and most important thing to find out is why. And not just the reasons given out in the first instance, either. You need to know the real reasons. Often the real reasons are easier to resolve than the superficial ones.

If your fiancé's parents say you're too 'high powered' the real reason might be that they feel intimidated by your success, so all you need to do is show them you can be an 'ordinary girl' in private, as well as an efficient executive at the office.

If your parents say your fiancé is 'pushy and rude' it could be that they find his ebullient personality a bit more lively than they're used to, and perhaps are afraid your fiancé will eclipse and dominate you once you're married. Explain this openly to your fiancé and ask him to take things easy with your parents, get to know them as individuals, and their fears could soon be reduced.

One or other set of parents may disapprove because they think you're too young. Now this may not seem like a very sympathetic thing to say, but are they right? Would it be that much of a problem for you to live together and wait a while before tying the knot? And I'm not suggesting you do that purely to please your parents. If you are very young, you are still growing, changing and evolving as people. It's worth taking plenty of time before marrying, to make sure you're both growing, changing and evolving in the same direction. (There speaks the voice of personal experience!)

Some parental disapproval can arise out of jealousy or even grief at the thought of 'losing' you. These often prove to be the underlying real reasons, camouflaged by more frivolous excuses. Here, providing love and reassurance on your part is terribly important, and provided you really mean it, is often a surprisingly easy way to solve the disapproval problem. (See also sections titled Fathers and Mothers.)

Bad-mouthing mother

My parents were absolutely against the wedding. They didn't like my fiancé, they didn't want us to be married in the church he and I were attending, they didn't approve of our choice of bridesmaids because two were not of our race.

Mom called my future mother-in-law, six weeks before the wedding, to tell her that my future husband was making 'the worst mistake of his life. He'll live to regret it. She's not good enough for him.' It was a long, ugly, one-sided conversation.

To top it off, my parents had eloped when they were married. So Mom micromanaged every detail, wanting to make my wedding the perfect event she missed out on.

Then, of course, she told us that because of their reservations, they would pay for none of it and would not attend. When we didn't freak out over that one, they reversed themselves.

Our response was to cave in on just about everything. What mattered to us was to end the day married, to have the ceremony in the church we attended, and to include my close friends as bridesmaids. Other than those things, we let my mother do whatever she wanted. It ended up feeling like her wedding, certainly, but it kept *her* screaming, crying phone calls to a minimum.

I also moved into my mother-in-law's house for about five weeks before the wedding: because she was mortified that my mom was badmouthing me, she offered me a safer place to stay. I was grateful.

Eighteen years and four children later, Mom actually likes my husband. She still would love to micromanage our lives, but that's not happening. And she still doesn't understand why my mother-in-law dislikes her.

Christine, Maryland, USA

P

85

Divorced parents

Nowadays more and more couples who get divorced manage to do so on reasonably friendly terms, which makes getting everyone together for your wedding relatively easy. Most of the wedding etiquette books and websites nowadays offer advice on how to handle seating plans, reception lines, etc when you have a gaggle of parents and step-parents to accommodate, so I won't duplicate all that here.

However if you're unlucky and your divorced parents – or your fiancé's – happen to hate each other, don't worry. Once again, remember that you are no longer shackled by tradition, and so you must not let yourself be forced into making uncomfortable choices that will affect your own happiness and enjoyment of the day. Sometimes you just can't help the antics of warring divorced parents, but with my favourite lateral thinking there is always a way around the problem; see Anya's contribution, below.

Helpful alternative

My sister, the bride, asked me to give the 'bride's father's' speech, as the best solution to the perennial problem of divorced parents. In short, the bride's mother refused to come if the bride's father gave the speech, and the bride's father was embarrassed and upset by the first solution suggested, that the mother's brother give a speech. In the midst of a family crisis my sister called me in floods of tears to ask me to do it, and of course I agreed.

Anya, London, UK

Divorced parents with new partners

If one or other of the divorced parents has since remarried, the usual etiquette is that the new spouse must be invited to the wedding. I think less formalised relationships – i.e. live-in partners or girlfriends/boyfriends – can be handled according to how it will make other members of the family feel. If a new partner has been the obvious 'cause' of the parents' marriage break-up then out of respect to the injured party concerned it's best to invite only the other parent. If this causes resentment you can compensate, perhaps, by arranging to meet that parent plus the new partner for dinner or drinks soon after the wedding, for a private celebration.

If it's likely that friction will erupt into trouble on the reception line or at the head table of the wedding meal, once again use lateral thinking. Drop the reception line altogether; have a reception line consisting of just you and the groom, or perhaps you, the groom, and your mothers while your fathers and step-fathers mingle with the guests. If you fear that bread rolls could get thrown in anger at the head table, drop the traditional head table idea and place the parents in question appropriately at tables of their own around the space. Then have a table for bride, groom and bridal attendants instead (probably more fun anyway.)

Never forget that there are alternatives, and don't be afraid to use them. Always remember whose day it is.

Carefully brief the wedding vendors

I was a wedding photographer for 18 years, and have really seen everything.

Probably one of the greatest difficulties is having divorced parents that don't get along. I've been to weddings where it's hard to get the mom and dad into the church together – they don't want to be anywhere near each other, even at their child's wedding. This puts a huge stress on the child. One way to alleviate this problem is to have the bride and groom talk to each of the wedding vendors ahead of time. If you talk to the photographer, she won't try and put the parents into the same photograph. The wedding coordinator won't put the parents together by the bride and groom during the toast. Wedding vendors have a lot of suggestions for handling situations, so it's important for a bride and groom to share their concerns ahead of time.

Lori Osterberg
Colorado, USA
www.VirtualPhotographyStudio.com
Lori@VisionOfSuccess.com

P

Step-versus birth parents

Another delicate issue can arise if you find yourself closer to a step-parent than the equivalent birth parent.

With mothers it isn't so much of a problem because they are unlikely to have any clear-cut expectations about who should help you organise the wedding, and that duty will fall naturally to the person you are closer to and spend more time with. As for the etiquette of seating at the ceremony and the reception, my advice would be to place whichever person you feel closer to in the role of mother of the bride. Once again, it's your day and there's no way I feel anyone should have to pander to someone they don't care for purely on the basis of familial rank.

With fathers, traditions are more exacting and if you want to follow them, you may well be expected to make a choice between step- and birth fathers to walk you down the aisle and make the speech. Don't be forced into making that choice unless you want to. Alternatives here include getting one father to do the walking, the other to do the talking; getting someone else (see above) to walk you; walking down with your groom, or by yourself. Ask them each to make a speech; ask someone else to do the father-of-the-bride speech (it doesn't have to be a man – it could be your mother, sister or even the maid/matron of honour).

Also see section titled Speeches.

Photography

As photography – particularly wedding photography – is not my strongest skill, I asked two professional wedding photographers, Yakir Zur and Geoff Beattie, to advise us on this topic. So here goes.

P

The problems: advice from a professional wedding photographer

You hear all kinds of horror stories about wedding photography. Some stories are about rude and unprofessional photographers, or poor quality photographs or clients who discovered on the morning of their wedding that the photographer is a total stranger and not the one they have signed for the wedding. You also hear stories about clients who decide after the wedding that they are quite happy with the snaps that their friends took during the wedding and refuse to pay the photographer. In order to avoid these horrible situations we should be aware of the potential pitfalls. The main problem is as always due to miscommunication. We also have to be aware of false presentation and unrealistic expectations.

The wedding photography market is a very competitive one with many photographers fighting for a share in a relatively shrinking market. Like in many other professions there are a few who are giving the entire profession a bad name. Be aware of the 'cowboys'.

Glamour images of brides which appear in various wedding magazines and publications can create unrealistic expectations among clients. Eventually this can lead to a feeling of being let down by the photographer when their wedding photos do not resemble these glamour images. Understanding the nature of wedding photography and the difference between photographing a model in a studio and photographing a wedding in real time is necessary in order to avoid disappointment.

Yakir Zur LBPPA
Hertfordshire, UK
www.yzphotography.co.uk

How to avoid problems

I asked Yakir to give us some advice on how to choose an appropriate photographer.

How to pick the right person: advice from a professional wedding photographer

Be clear about what you are looking for and realistic about what you can get for the money you are willing to spend. £500 won't get you a 'David Bailey' even if the photographer swears to you that he is the next best thing, but that doesn't mean that you have to break the bank to have some decent photos from your wedding day. Decide what your maximum budget is for a photographer and stick to it. Make sure that you understand the full cost of the package and don't ask for extra service without asking how much extra it will cost you. Today's fashionable digitally printed book albums look fantastic, but they are expensive and can sometimes double the cost of your wedding photography.

Shop around; look on photographers' websites and make a shortlist of those whose work you like. If you like contemporary design and photography don't choose a traditional photographer; but if you like the traditional style, avoid the journalistic style photographer.

Check which one of them is within your price range and book an appointment to see more of their work. Try and view a full set of proofs from at least one wedding and never rely only on the images you've seen on the website. If you are dealing with a big studio, make sure that the photographer whose work you see is the one who'll show up on your doorstep on the morning of your wedding day. If you are dealing with a single photographer, ask them if they have a contingency plan in case they are unable to work on that day. Check if they are a member of a professional photographers' association (like the BIPP, BPPA, SWPP and the MPA). This is always a good indication as to the level of his/her professionalism. However there are many good photographers who aren't members of an organisation but can produce a very good body of work.

P

Get to know the photographer. Have a proper meeting with him/her and see if you like him/her as a person, not only their work. Personal rapport is one of the most important things in choosing a wedding photographer. You'll feel much more relaxed and at ease with someone you like and it will show in the photos.

When planning your wedding day, make sure you leave enough time for the photographer. I tend to have the last meeting with the couple no more than couple of weeks before the wedding where we discuss the details and make sure that there are enough time slots for the photographer. On the other hand, don't let the photographer ruin your day by bossing you around. This is your special day and you deserve to be treated with respect.

Yakir Zur LBPPA
Hertfordshire, UK
www.yzphotography.co.uk

What you need to do

Although a good wedding photographer will handle almost every aspect of this important task him or herself, there are several things you can do to help him or her, and so ensure you all get the best possible result. Geoff takes up the story.

Co-operating with the photographer, the key to a good result: advice from a professional wedding photographer

P

Planning and style

It's essential you choose the right style of photographer – traditional or contemporary. A traditional style photographer would not be able to create you a contemporary album in the same way a contemporary photographer would.

Co-operate

Work with the photographer on the day and ask your guests to as well. A photographer can't get happy smiling wedding photos of the guests if they are all miserable and won't smile or co-operate with the photographer when prompted, especially with group shots! A common example would be that people in the group aren't looking at the camera! It's not the photographer's fault, all photographers will ask everyone in the group to look at the camera for the group shots, though people often don't and later on the photographer will get the blame! Many things can now be corrected digitally, but it's always better to get things right in the first place.

List

Do a list of shots you want and don't want, be sure to inform the photographer of this. Even if you want a contemporary style album, the photographer will (or should) always accommodate your requests, especially if Uncle John and Auntie Andrea are travelling halfway around the world to be at your wedding with the new baby and you want a shot with them.

Location

Choose the location carefully for posed group shots. Most photographers should know the best locations for photos. If you are getting married in a location without a photogenic background, arrange with the driver to detour on the way to your reception.

Time scale

Check before you book how long the whole package takes to complete and get back into your hands.

Insurance

Does the photographer offer you or include any insurance? If not, this is available from some insurance companies, in some cases to cover the cost of a complete reshoot!

Force majeure and illness

What's the backup plan? Do they have any cover available?

Take lots of photos

Remember – you can't go back and re-do wedding photos! Take lots and get your guests to take lots too.

Geoff Beattie
Creative Photo Shop and Portrait Studio
Wigan, UK
www.creativephotoshop.co.uk

P

Keep the photo session short

After the ceremony at a friend's wedding the wedding party took so much time taking photos that the guests (especially those like me who didn't know each other very well, so found it hard to 'mingle') were at the end of our tethers by the time the wedding party regrouped for the meal and speeches. It would have been great to just sneak away, but instead we had to grit our teeth and stay put, so as not to appear rude.

Kay Mussellwhite, UK

Using an amateur – is it worth the risk?

Unless you're really up against it for money, I would say don't take the risk of leaving all the photography to an amateur. However, amateurs can get some excellent shots, particularly of the impromptu, unposed style and often it's nice to have a combination of the formal, professional pictures with some informal snaps as well.

If amateurs offer to take pictures, by all means accept, for this reason. Also, you may find that the professional photographer does not include pictures of the reception in the package; this is where the shots done by amateurs can fill in conveniently.

DIY wedding photographs – professional advice
Please note that Geoff Beattie, one of the two professional photographers who contributed here, offers a useful eBook, *DIY Wedding Photo Tips and Guide* which you can download from his website, www.creativephotoshop.co.uk

---

Postponement or Cancellation

Do you need to tell people why?

No, you don't, but unless the reason is particularly sensitive it is kinder to give some sort of explanation. Postponements are more often done for reasons outside of the bride's and groom's personal relationship and as such can be slightly less personal to share, e.g. a family bereavement, illness, etc. In that case it's fair enough to make the point. But if the wedding is to be cancelled because the bride and groom have split up, that's no one else's business. Just informing people that the wedding has been cancelled should be enough for them to work that out for themselves.

How do you tell them?

This really depends on how much time there is available. If there is still quite a long lead time you can simply have some cards printed and mailed out to the guest list, saying words to the effect of:

- *Cancellation: The marriage arranged between John Doe and Mary Smith will now not take place.*

- *Postponement: Due to a family bereavement the marriage between John Doe and Mary Smith has been postponed until further notice.*

- *Postponement: Due to the bride's recent car accident, the marriage between John Doe and Mary Smith has been postponed until Saturday, XX Month, 20XX, at 11am at Anytown Register Office and afterwards at Anytown House Hotel.*

If there isn't time to get cards printed and mailed (and don't forget any overseas guests who might have fairly elaborate travel plans to rearrange), then it's phone calls and emails. Informing people of bad news like this by email is a lot easier on you than having to have 100 + identical telephone conversations during which you're asked questions you'd rather not answer.

However not everyone has access to email and even people who do often forget to look at theirs, so you may have to resort to phone calls for some. If you're upset about the postponement or cancellation, don't put yourself through the wringer. Get a family member or friend to make the calls for you and also, possibly, send the emails, so you don't get a flood of sympathetic replies that will only remind you of what you're going through.

Local or national newspaper

If your engagement and/or wedding was announced in the local paper or one of the national broadsheets in the UK, you may also want to place a notice in there now, with wording similar to that of the printed cards I describe above.

Reception and other costs

If there is plenty of time in hand you shouldn't be too heavily penalised by ceremony and reception venues, photographers, caterers, etc and in many cases you should be able to get at least part of your deposits back from them. This is especially relevant in the case of a postponement where you can rebook the facilities and suppliers at the same time, so assuring them that they will still get your business eventually.

And another point – don't forget to cancel or postpone your honeymoon as soon as possible, too.

Wedding insurance

Wedding insurance usually covers you for any unforeseen reason why the wedding can't go ahead, but from what I can see most policies *do not* cover you if bride or groom change their mind and break it off. You'll find plenty of information about wedding insurance if you key **wedding insurance** into Google or another search engine or look up the Wedding Guide in your local *Yellow Pages*. Also see section titled Wedding Insurance.

Return all gifts

This is the really hard part – sending all the gifts back if your wedding has been cancelled. Some people, especially close friends and family, might tell you to keep their gift, especially if you've already started to use it. However as all the etiquette books and websites will tell you, those gifts have got to go back – with a note thanking the person and explaining briefly why they're getting it back. If you have a large number of gifts I would have thought it's OK to have a printed note so all you have to do is sign each personally. Writing 150 letters all about the break-up of your engagement is not something I would inflict on anyone.

What about your dress?

Once again much depends on how far along the track you've got with it. If you've ordered a standard design in a fairly common size, you might be able to do a deal with the store concerned whereby they sell it on so you can recoup at least some of your investment.

Other alternatives include selling it on ebay (www.ebay.co.uk) or through placing an advertisement in your local newspaper or newsagent's shop, having it dyed another colour so you can use it as an evening dress, or keeping it – you might need it again one day!

What about the engagement ring?

This can be a controversial issue and there are many stories about brides-not-to-be angrily hurling five carat diamond engagement rings into open fires, rivers, oceans, traffic snarl-ups and various other unrecoverable places. However once again the etiquette books and websites mostly say that it should be returned, especially if it's the bride who has broken it off.

If the ring is a family heirloom then in all honesty it should go back to that family, whoever's it is. But in the case of the groom breaking it off, the etiquette isn't so clear. My personal inclination would be to sell the ring and spend the proceeds on a wonderful night out with my friends. But then … !!

Pregnancy

No more shotgun weddings

Except in very rare circumstances I think the days of the shotgun wedding are well and truly over, and that's a very good thing. That's not just because it avoids the illegal use of firearms, but also because it means the stigma of being pregnant out of wedlock is now firmly where it belongs – in the past.

Of course in some cultures and religions there still is a stigma about premarital pregnancy, but in most industrialised countries society has become far more comfortable with the idea than it was even in the mid-20th century. You might still get the occasional disapproving sniff (or worse – see 'Screenmom's' contribution below) but no longer will you get Pappy using his rabbit gun as a cattle-prod to get the groom up the aisle. At least I hope not.

So in these modern times the only issues that arise from being a pregnant bride are connected with practical things like when to get married, what to wear, and how the bride will feel at that particular stage of her pregnancy.

When to get married

That's a tricky one. A lot depends on whether:

- your pregnancy was planned or not
- you need to use the wedding money for the new baby
- you will feel up to organising a wedding while pregnant
- you want to wait until after the birth.

Let's look at the two main options. They're pretty simple: before, or after.

First, before: the advantages
- Your baby will be born 'in wedlock'.
- You will not be trying to organise a wedding with a young baby in tow.
- Your family – especially the older ones – might feel more comfortable with this.
- You can get away with a smaller, simpler, cheaper wedding than you might otherwise.

P

And now, before: the disadvantages

- You will be organising a wedding when you may not be feeling at your fittest.

- You will need to think carefully about what you will wear.

- Realistically you probably won't have as grand a wedding as you would have if not pregnant.

- You probably won't have as much money to spend on your wedding/ honeymoon.

- You may not be in a position to enjoy your honeymoon quite so much.

OK. Now, after: the advantages

- You can choose a date when your figure will have returned to normal.

- You can wear a dress that does not look like a tent.

- You should be feeling OK again provided your baby sleeps at night (some do, so I'm told ...).

- You can organise the wedding without the sensation of a meter running.

And after: the disadvantages

- Your baby will not have been born 'in wedlock'.

- You will be organising a wedding while caring for a young baby.

- You might just get some disapproval from certain family members.

- Your honeymoon may have to include baby too (not necessarily a disadvantage!).

Other alternatives

Fine. Those alternatives are the obvious ones. However if we lift ourselves out of the 'obvious box' there are some other possibilities you can consider.

For starters, you could split your wedding plans. In other words, have a small wedding – maybe just a register office do – while you're expecting your baby, then have a big reception or party after baby arrives and you're all feeling slim and fit again.

Assuming you have an understanding wedding officiant, you could even develop a religious blessing to be held at an appropriate time after your civil wedding – which could be combined with a baptism service for your baby. Then, you could move that on into a combined wedding and baptism reception.

So what do you do?

Where getting married before the birth is concerned, I would say let your pregnancy guide you. You will know fairly early on in your pregnancy whether you are going to be feeling nauseous or not. If you are, don't despair, as that usually dies down in the second trimester of pregnancy. However in your shoes I would avoid a wedding in the third trimester – especially the latter stages – because you may find standing and sitting and in fact everything (!!) somewhat uncomfortable. You may also feel very tired, very easily.

Talk to your doctor and your midwife. They know all about pregnancy and all about you, so are well qualified to advise on whether a wedding before the birth is a good idea or not.

Whatever happens, don't be panicked into making hasty decisions about getting married if/when/while you are pregnant. Keep calm and analyse everything carefully. Once again, never forget whose wedding it is. Even if others try to pressurise you into making a decision, consider what's best for you, your fiancé and your baby. You three matter most.

Pregnant pauses

During college I worked in a very busy flower shop. We did between three to six weddings every Saturday all year round due to the temperate climate. I have probably been to 100 weddings to set up flowers at the church, reception, home, etc. Out of 100 weddings I saw two (that's two) weddings go off in fairytale style. They were achingly beautiful. I still remember them even though this had to be 20 years ago.

Of the weddings that didn't go off in fairytale style, one is particularly memorable. I always got to the church at least 1 hour before the start of the ceremony, in case anything went wrong. In this case though, the second I got there, nothing was right. I was met at the door of the church by the bride who looked ready to give birth at that moment. She was in hysterics and her future mother-in-law came screaming after her. Before I could put my armload of flowers down, the mother of the groom had grabbed the bride to be by the hair and slapped her hard across the face. At *that* point the groom (I assume) pulls his mother off his future wife and catches her in a choke hold. At that point the groom's brother and best man (I assume) jumps on his brother (the groom) and begins to mutilate the man's face with his fist. All the while, the mother is screaming that the bride-to-be is an unholy whore and is not carrying her son's child but the spawn of the devil. The groom is screaming at his crazed mother that she has to shut her f*cking mouth or he will kill her. The brother is screaming that the mother is probably right and the groom is a disrespectful b*st*rd and always has been. The bride is just screaming incoherently.

It was the minister who brought the love fest to an end, but not before he got a stray punch to the eye. He got everyone separated and fairly calm. He told me to leave the flowers, but there would not be a ceremony that day. He couldn't bring himself to marry a couple who had just been duking it out in the vestibule of the church with close family members. As I was leaving the police pulled up.

Doncha' love love?

'Screenmom,' USA

Your dress

This may be an obvious one, but if you're pregnant, when choosing or commissioning your dress make sure you allow for the stage of pregnancy at which you will be on the date of the wedding. Empire line designs are very useful here. Some designs can hide an early pregnancy very effectively, but many women these days are proud to share their bump with all and sundry. If so, let the design of your dress show that.

Others' pregnancies

Baby wouldn't wait

Our wedding planner/co-ordinator fell pregnant after we appointed her ... the baby was due the week after our wedding. We liked her a lot and she assured us that there'd be no problems with working when she was nearing full term.

She ended up having to go into hospital the day before our wedding, so we had to run around at the last minute with a few collections/deliveries.

As she was a sole operator/freelancer, the only thing she could do on the day was to send her mum, who was lovely, but didn't really have much of a clue.

Resolution? Well, we just got on and did things. We were a bit cross about being left in the lurch, but couldn't be that harsh on her as she was in hospital (mother and baby were fine in the end).

Steve Wilson
Hallmark Public Relations Ltd, UK
www.hallmarkpr.com

Finally, be mindful of pregnant ladies among your wedding guests – don't expect them to stand around for too long, and allocate somewhere comfortable for them to sit.

Pre-nuptial Agreements

There is a lot of controversy over pre-nuptial agreements, particularly in terms of how enforceable they really are in legal terms.

Taking a romantic view of it, you shouldn't really need one. However the reality is that in certain – albeit fairly rare – circumstances, a pre-nuptial agreement is a sensible precaution. As it is something of a legal minefield I asked UK solicitor Sue McGaughran to give us her views on the topic and how things stand currently in the UK.

Pre-nuptial/pre-marriage agreements: advice from UK solicitor Sue McGaughran

We associate them mainly with celebrity marriages, because for years celebrities have been given legal advice about protecting their assets on marriage. That advice includes setting a limit on divorce pay out. You don't, however, have to be a celebrity. If you are looking to protect your assets on marriage there is protection available regardless of how you earn your salary. Whilst the divorce rate in the UK seems to be slightly decreasing from the all-time high in 2002, there were still over 141,000 divorces in 2005. Marriage is no longer until death do us part so it pays to look at where the law currently stands.

What is a pre-nuptial agreement?

Effectively this is an agreement between two people, before they marry; it sets out how their assets will be dealt with on divorce. Currently the majority of agreements drafted relate to marriage and divorce. Increasingly those couples wanting to live together and share their lives also want to deal with the potential financial exposure on breakdown of that relationship (often called a Pre-relationship Agreement) and those entering into Civil Partnerships are looking to enter into similar agreements (often called a Pre-Civil Partnership Agreement).

The agreement can deal with all and any assets from the home the couple live in, to who will get what part of the CD collection, or the pets.

Is a pre-nuptial agreement binding in the UK?

Unfortunately, whilst in many States in the USA pre-nuptial agreements are binding on individuals as the marriage breaks up, it is not yet quite the same in the UK, although many feel that the UK will eventually follow USA law. Previously the UK courts, when dealing with a divorce, gave little consideration to a pre-nuptial agreement. Now the courts are taking them into consideration.

To determine how closely the terms of the agreement are adhered to the court will now consider:

- Was there a full and frank disclosure of both parties' financial circumstances and assets before they entered into the agreement?

- How long before the wedding was the agreement signed? (Obviously the court won't want it to be on the wedding day, because it may reflect pressure on one or both parties.)

- If it was some time before the wedding, they will consider whether since the agreement, but before the marriage, the financial circumstances of one party changed (e.g. a salary increase, one party took a career break to care for the parties' child, etc); ideally not less than 21 days before the wedding but not more than about three months before either.

- Following on from above, what significant changes have there been since the agreement was signed? for example again salary increase, etc, but also the length of the marriage and the health and wealth (e.g. one party inherited from parents) of both parties.

- Was any pressure (emotional or financial) placed on either party before they signed the agreement? (Pressure could be from the other party, but could also be from relatives, etc, too.)

- Did both parties or either party get any independent legal advice before they entered into the agreement? (There is likely to be less consideration of the agreement by the court if one party did and the other did not.)

Increasingly the existence of a pre-nuptial agreement will influence any Order that a Court makes on the dissolution of a marriage or breakdown of a relationship.

Why?

Even though they are not binding on the UK court increasingly people are entering into them because they are seen as a protective measure.

They can help protect:

i)   a family business

ii) children

iii) assets from a previous marriage

iv) assets in another country

v)   the marriage by laying down the financial expectations with full disclosure at the outset.

What can I put in the agreement?

The agreement can cover anything sensible including:

1 How both parties' income will be dealt with during the marriage and who will pay for what.

2 How any debts the parties have before the marriage will be dealt with.

3 Dealing with the assets that the parties owned before marriage, etc.

4 What will happen to any home the parties live in.

5 What will happen to any joint savings.

6 What will happen to any furniture.

7 What will happen to any life insurances and pensions.

As an example, some of the 'celebrity' agreements include clauses about:

1 Cheating and what will happen if one party does cheat.

2 An equal share of housework .

Some more bizarre clauses (which we would not really recommend) include clauses about

1 not leaving the toilet seat up

2 equal control of the remote controls to TV, DVD, etc.

How do we get one?

Step 1

Ideally, both parties need to sit down and discuss what they want to do. There needs to be a full and frank disclosure from both parties of their financial circumstances and assets before they draft the agreement. It is also wise to include your life-plans here; such as if the parties intend to have or adopt children, is one party taking a career break, etc?

Step 2

Draft out in basic non-legal terms what you both agree and maybe a brief explanation why, e.g. we want the house in which we are living at the time we split up to be sold, the mortgage, any legal charges on it, and all expenses to be paid out of the sale proceeds and then the left-over money to be split as to A 40% and B 60% because B alone paid the deposit on the house of £10,000.

Step 3

You can then draft the agreement yourself although it would be wise to either:

i) use a template document – there will be some things you forget and the template may serve as a prompt or

ii) get an agreement professionally drafted.

Step 4

We recommend that you either both get independent legal advice on that draft agreement, or you both agree not to. The latter may be acceptable where the assets are small and the agreement is very straightforward.

Step 5

The agreement can then be signed by both of you and you both keep a copy.

Sue McGaughran
Solicitor, Lime One Ltd
www.limeone.co.uk

Please note Sue's advice is up to date as at November 2006. Laws and circumstances regarding pre-nuptial agreements may change over time, so check the current position with Sue, or with your own legal advisers.

P

Reception Lines

At a large wedding it can take a long time for everyone to pass down the line and be greeted by the bride, groom, their parents, etc. In the meantime guests often are expected to stand around waiting, sometimes outdoors, and can get bored, tired and thirsty.

If you're going to have a formal wedding reception line like this it's far kinder to your guests to arrange for them to stand in relative comfort and have drinks passed around to them before they go along the line to shake hands and kiss everyone.

You might risk the odd bit of spilled wine here and there, but your guests will appreciate not having been lined up for 30 minutes or more like sheep waiting to go through a de-lousing dip.

Alternatives can include holding the receiving line in a side room, so people are not obliged to queue, restricting the receiving line merely to the bride and groom, and dispensing with it altogether in favour of the bride and groom circulating fairly around all tables during the reception.

Register Offices

See sections titled Civil Weddings, and Civil Partnerships.

Rehearsals and Rehearsal Dinners

Wedding rehearsals are a key element of reducing stress and uncertainty on the day, particularly if your ceremony is religious and involves complex procedures. Whatever you do, don't be tempted to gloss over the rehearsal; it will help you enormously on the day to know what's expected and, far more important, to help you and your groom to enjoy the experience without uncertainty.

In theory you should have your wedding rehearsal a day or two before the event. If you have relatives and other key participants arriving from abroad, you should try to ensure that they arrive in plenty of time for the rehearsal so they will be comfortable with what is expected of them.

Rehearsal dinners are considered very important in North America because they are, in many cases, the first time both sides of the family-to-be are brought together to get to know one another. In the UK and Europe rehearsal dinners aren't always considered as such an important part of the wedding rigmarole, but increasingly they seem to be climbing up the popularity stakes.

And if nothing else, the rehearsal dinner can provide the opportunity for a very, very good party!

Relatives, Other

R

Elderly relatives

There isn't a more proud moment for a grandparent or great-grandparent than to see their loved one get married. Unlike your parents, who may have issues about the 'rite of passage' and the thought of losing you to a stranger, grandparents and other elderly relatives seem to view it merely as a delight-ful milestone. It's very important to them to be able to share your day with you and usually they will go to some lengths to be there, even if it's difficult for them to travel and move around.

If there is one or more older person who is in any way disabled coming to your wedding, you will need to ensure they can access both the ceremony and reception venues as easily as possible. You'll also want to make sure they get the best seat in the house, so they can see everything clearly.

At the reception, if they are hard of hearing try to seat them in as quiet a location as possible. Even with efficient hearing aids, trying to pick up a conversation when there is a lot of ambient noise is very difficult for them.

Even if they can hear well and are physically fit, elderly people tire very quickly. It's essential that you provide somewhere comfortable for them to sit at times when everyone else is standing – e.g. during the reception line or drinks before the meal. It's also worth getting someone to stand by to take them home relatively early on during the reception. They may not like to ask for this to be done, but probably will be very grateful to find that they can slip away quietly when their energy begins to flag.

Aunts, uncles, cousins

Most relatives that are not immediate family are quite happy to muck in with other (unrelated) guests, but sometimes you'll get one or two who very much want to participate on a more involved level.

Rather than view this as a potential nuisance, you might well find they have hidden talents which could be very useful, like a knowledge of local live bands or DJs, flower arranging, dress making, cake baking, etc. Be positive and think creatively here, and you could add an extremely useful person to your team.

Relatives coming from abroad

Even if you haven't seen Auntie Madge since you were a little girl, if she and her hubby make the effort and go to the expense of flying over from Singapore to attend your wedding, you really should treat them specially.

If they arrive a few days before the wedding, try to create a slot in your schedule to stop by and say hello to them, even if it is only for a quick cup of coffee. Then make sure that someone mentions them in their wedding speech, thanking them for coming all that way.

Rings

There's not a lot to say about worries associated with rings, really, other than all the jokes about the best man dropping them down the toilet just before the ceremony ... but OK, yes, I do have a couple of things I'd like to point out to you!

Of course, you may well have decided on wedding ring designs that would fit in with your engagement ring, and that's all well and good.

But here are some cold, hard facts about wedding rings and your fingers which may influence your buying decision.

1. You may not always remain the same ring size. Over the years circumstances, menopause and other issues will crop up and could well result in your wedding ring becoming too tight/too loose, or whatever.

2. You may acquire further important rings as time goes on, other than your engagement ring (most women wear that above their wedding ring).

Solution? Well, in your shoes I would choose a slim wedding band which can accommodate whatever extra choices you decide to add later. A wide-banded wedding ring, although stylish in the first instance, will make you look like you're wearing knuckle-dusters later on should you add your engagement ring and an eternity ring on top of it. Also, should you put on weight or experience any swelling of your hands (e.g. during pregnancy) a wide wedding band will be very uncomfortable, and will be difficult to have enlarged. A narrow, plain wedding band that sits at the base of your finger should be comfortable even if you put on a few kilos, and it can be enlarged – by a jeweller, of course – quite easily and cheaply.

Quality – carat content isn't necessarily best

Many jewellers will tell you that the higher the gold carat content of the ring, the better it is. In a way that's true. However in real terms I believe things are somewhat different.

Let's take a quick look at the way gold is processed here in the UK and in most other western cultures.

Pure gold is 24 carat – very beautiful, but very soft. To make it harder it's normally allied with one or more of a number of different other metals including brass, nickel, copper and various others. The degree to which this dilution takes place results in the different 'carat' measurements you'll see in the hallmark of gold jewellery.

Alloying gold with these other metals tends to make the end product harder and more resilient. Essentially, the lower the 'carat' content of gold, the harder the piece will be.

If the jeweller concerned tries to sell you 18 carat or even 22 carat gold wedding rings, bear in mind that although you'd be right in assuming the gold is a lot nearer pure gold, also it will be very soft and liable to scratching, dulling, and eventually, wearing thin.

Ironically, cheaper is better here, because 14, 10 and 9 carat gold rings will last you longer than the purer types, and will keep their looks better.

Platinum and other precious metals

Platinum and its associates are often much valued, although I'm not sure why. Platinum wedding rings are very lightweight, but are somewhat more difficult and expensive to alter should that need arise in the future.

My recommendation (as the co-author of *The Jewellery Book* some years ago) is to go for 9 or 14 carat gold, either white or coloured.

R

Seating Plans

So how do you organise them?

These days the online environment is full of useful programmes that allow you to experiment with placement of names on forms and all manner of devices that supposedly sort anything up to thousands of items into a beautifully homogenised final product.

That's all fine and dandy. But with weddings, often you're dealing with people and issues who are not necessarily up with the latest computer-based sorting techniques and will look at you as if you're drooling mad should you suggest something so outlandishly technical. In any case, using a computer programme to sort out the seating plan for your reception could well end up being more complex than doing it the good old-fashioned way.

Here's an extremely low tech, but nonetheless useful idea for sorting out your seating plan.

Get a large sheet of paper (old, redundant rolls of wallpaper are handy for this) and spread it out. Draw on it the tables you envisage bearing in mind the total number of guests.

Write the names of all your guests on a list, then cut that up so each name is on its own scrap of paper.

Place the master plan on a large space like a dining table or a spare floor, and use the small scraps to represent each guest. You are free to move everyone around at this stage! So use your discretion appropriately and then formulate a final seating plan on that basis.

What, who and where?

Some people think they should be clever and divide their guests up into tables according to all manner of ideas. This can work. Also, it can be a disaster.

Having asked quite a few of my friends and contacts the question, 'What did you find the most challenging part of organising your/your daughter's wedding?' the almost unanimous response was, 'The seating plan.'

If you are determined to have a wedding feast at which people are sat at relatively small tables by designation (rather than as they choose if you have a free-ranging buffet meal) then there are a few issues you should take into consideration.

For starters, forget trying to be *avant garde* and mix up guests by splitting them up from their partners and sitting them next to total strangers. This may work at boozy dinner parties on an entirely informal basis, but – hey – do you want that type of challenge at your wedding?

If you have a wide ranging mix of guests most of whom don't know each other, it helps a lot to appoint one key friend or family member to sit at each table, having been briefed on who is sitting there, to help break the ice and get the conversations going. It also helps to try to group together guests who may have similar interests (e.g. children the same age, similar interests, related jobs).

What about family members?

This is where seating plans can get hugely complex. At most weddings there has to be a 'top table' at which the key dignitaries of the day are sat, usually in a predetermined pecking order. This is fine if everyone gets along OK, but can be hell on wheels if there are social or domestic issues.

Most of the wedding websites and wedding planning books tell you how to deal with divorced and step-family members when arranging your seating plan, so I won't bore you with all that again here. However when you read those passages informing you of the etiquette you should observe when mum doesn't talk to dad and step-mum can't stand your sister and your brother has threatened to annihilate the best man for speaking inappropriately about your waistline, don't worry.

Use your commonsense and seat people according to what *you* feel is right. Never, never under-estimate your own instincts and ability to see what really matters, irrespective of how much pressure you might feel under to behave differently. As I've said repeatedly in this book and feel no shame in repeating here – do *not* forget whose wedding it is.

Second Marriages

For second marriages here we should really read 'second and subsequent' marriages, as some of us have gone beyond number two and are heading slowly towards the double figures (OK, in my case, only just!). So if you're looking at your third or fourth or whatever, please don't be offended by my simplification of the topic down to 'second weddings'. It just makes it tidier this way.

One thing I must get off my chest here is the term 'remarriage.' Most people use this term to describe the ceremony when people get married again. However to me, being the boring pedant that I am, the word remarriage suggests getting married again to the person you were previously married to prior to a divorce – which of course does happen. OK, rant over.

Generally speaking second marriages are less elaborate affairs, although if one or the other party – especially the bride – has not been married before, the whole event can be just as elaborate as a first marriage.

The key issues

There are quite a few issues that differentiate second marriages from first marriages. Most of them are very obvious: exes, children, step-families-to-be, ex-in-laws-who-are-nonetheless-grandparents, etc.

If you're marrying for the second time you may well be older than the average blushing bride and may have been living together for some time in a well established home, rather than just be starting out in a new household.

One delightful aspect of a second marriage is that even if the first time around you felt obliged to stick to traditions, this time you really are free to do whatever you like. Yes, there will be some restrictions on you such as not being able to have a religious ceremony in some circumstances, and possibly having a slightly more complex task ahead of you in organising your reception seating plan.

However with a second marriage, the expectations of family and friends are nothing like as fixed as they are for a first marriage. Some people say that their second wedding is actually what they would have liked to do for their first, but couldn't ... for reasons apart from who they were marrying, of course!

Attendants

Should you have bridesmaids, maid or matron of honour, a best man, ushers, etc when either one or both of you have been married before?

The answer to that might well be dictated by the nature of the wedding itself. If there is to be a religious ceremony or a civil ceremony in a grand location, with a large number of guests, you could probably justify having at least a bridesmaid or two and a best man. In any case you'll need two witnesses for your signing of the register; however these do not need to be a best man and a bridesmaid.

You'll also need a witness each if you're marrying in a register office. And although it might seem a cute romantic notion to haul two total strangers in off the street to witness your signatures, the reality would probably be disappointing.

Another thing to consider here is that with second and subsequent weddings you're not expected to follow traditions in the same way as you can be for your first. That opens up your choice. What about your parents? Your children?

Also see sections titled Best Man and Ushers, and Bridesmaids, Flower Girls and Pages.

Gifts

I've already covered this topic in the section titled Gifts and Gift Lists so will only recap here. Some people feel that you shouldn't expect gifts second time around, but many of your friends and family will want to give you something anyway.

Bear in mind that you don't need to have the usual range of gifts that are appropriate for a couple trying to equip their first home together; chances are you probably have all you need already. If you don't, then by all means suggest that people buy you household items, and if you want to, you can set up a wedding list at your favourite store or through a specialised service. To find that either key **wedding lists** into Google or another search engine, or look it up in the Wedding Guide of your local *Yellow Pages*.

Also bear in mind that instead of asking people for gifts, you can arrange for them to make contributions towards the cost of your honeymoon, or even make contributions to a charity of your choice.

Giving the bride away

This may be somewhat superfluous because the religious ceremonies in which a bride is given away are mainly not relevant to second marriages anyway. However there are certain circumstances in which a religious service is possible.

If the circumstances are such that the bride is to be given away, there is nothing to say that it has to be your father. In fact there may be reasons why you feel it's inappropriate to walk down the aisle with your father a second time. How about your brother, cousin, uncle or son? Mother, sister, daughter, best friend? Or walk by yourself? Or with your groom?

Now, even more than in the case of a first wedding, you're free to choose an alternative that suits you; the old, traditional obligations can be disregarded.

Guests

As far as close family members are concerned, you'll find I've touched on relevant issues in several other places in this book under appropriate headings. So let me just recap here.

Depending on your circumstances you may need to use some tact in terms of who you invite, especially if your previous marriage (or your groom's) has ended on less than friendly terms. You might just be unlucky and find yourself in a position whereby parties A and B will refuse to attend your wedding if parties C and D are present, or any one of a number of other uncomfortable permutations.

My feeling on this is, OK – you should try to persuade everyone who matters to you to attend your second wedding. However if it looks like turning the day into World War Three, sit back and remember whose wedding it is, and who will end up having this day spoiled by warring factions.

Instead of bending over backwards to reconcile differences that are probably irreconcilable anyway, suggest that parties A and B avoid the wedding and meet you shortly afterwards for drinks or dinner and a private celebration. At the end of the day it is their problem, not yours, and it is *not* your duty to headbang the whole thing on their behalf. You have more important, and more pleasant, things to do.

Invitations

The wording of printed invitations for second weddings often gives rise to uncertainty, because in this case there isn't the same sort of traditional etiquette to fall back on as there is with a first wedding.

For a reasonable solution, let's look at who is funding the exercise.

If it is the bridal couple themselves, then it's easy:

> *John Doe and Mary Smith invite (name) to their wedding at (place) on (date), etc.*

If the parents are paying, then either:

> *Mr and Mrs James Doe and Mr and Mrs Robert Brown invite (name) to the wedding of John and Mary at (place) on (date), etc.*

If you're all sharing the cost, how about:

> *Mr and Mrs James Doe, Mr John Doe, Mr and Mrs Robert Brown, Ms Mary Smith, invite (name) to John and Mary's wedding at (place) on (date), etc.*

And you could even involve your children on the invitation, which can go a long way towards smoothing over any wrinkles in upcoming step-relationships (also see section titled Children: second/subsequent marriages).

> *Mr John Doe, Laura and Stephanie Doe, Ms Mary Smith, James and Jonathan Smith, invite (name) to John and Mary's wedding at (place) on (date), etc.*

S

Planning

There really shouldn't be too many problems with the planning of a second wedding that you won't have experienced at your first, unless the politics of your relationship involve difficulties with family members – and even that can be dealt with using tact, diplomacy, and if all else fails, pulling rank and reminding everyone just whose wedding it is.

If you are busy with the rest of your day-to-day life and are intending to have a large wedding, you might want to consider hiring a wedding planner: see the section titled Wedding Planners.

Relatives

As always, good, clear communication is the healthiest way forward. You may find some of your relatives are disappointed that your previous marriage failed, and so are disinclined to view your impending next marriage in a favourable light. That may mean you have to work harder to show your loved ones that this marriage is very important to you and your future. Clear communication – honest talking at a deep level – will go a long way towards resolving any misunderstandings.

As you progress through the relatives (and close friends, whose opinions are important too) in my view it's critical that you don't lose sight of why you're doing this in the first place. By all means address a sceptical relative's concerns, but don't let them make you become neurotic and start re-examining all your own motives.

The key here? Before you tell anyone, be sure yourself. That way you will persuade most of the sceptics among your circle of family and friends and, where it comes to those who might remain unpersuaded, you will have sufficient courage of your own convictions not to care.

Religious services

This is pretty simple: check with your religious leader how s/he feels about second marriages. If s/he says no, ask her/him what the alternatives are.

The answer will vary enormously according to your religion and also according to your religion's current policies on 'remarriage'.

If your particular religion does not allow a second marriage, bear in mind that it may permit a blessing after a register office wedding, which can be almost as meaningful.

What to wear

The tradition of the bride's wearing of white harks back to a number of old-fashioned traditions including that of the idea that the white of the bridal gown represents her virginity. Well, I don't know about you, but to me – speaking as someone from a Western culture – that notion is a weensie bit outdated.

As the bride in a second marriage, you can wear what you like. Aren't you the lucky girl! If you want, you can tramline first-wedding traditions by wearing outfits that recall those of first marriages, but with a lot more grunt; look back at the outfits worn by the UK's Duchess of Cornwall to her husband the Prince of Wales on their wedding day. She looked outstanding, in my view. If you have an internet connection you should be able to see examples of her outfits by keying **Charles and Camilla** into Google or another search engine.

Siblings

Why do some siblings suddenly become antipathetic when you announce your engagement?

Of course, your own siblings may be delighted at the prospect of your getting married, but don't be surprised if you meet a certain attitude here and there that seems less enthusiastic than it should be.

Especially (but not necessarily) in very close families, the sudden emerging of one member out of the familial chrysalis into a new, married life – well, frankly, rocks the boat, particularly if you are the first of the family to take that step. Whether anyone likes it or not, the nature of your relationship with your siblings is going to change when you get married, no matter how much they may like your fiancé.

Your siblings, who previously perceived that they could have you all to themselves when they needed to, now face the fact that you will soon come ready-packed with a spouse. And worst of all for them, that spouse will take precedence in your eyes. Your siblings see themselves potentially being sidelined.

Your marriage is a right of passage that affects everyone in your family, and some siblings find this hard to deal with. Maybe it's because it makes them face the fact that your family is growing up; that the old childhood unity that provided such endearing security for you all is somehow being ruptured.

Whatever it is, though, the change that's facing you all can manifest itself in many different ways among your siblings – from apparent disinterest in your wedding to spiteful, nasty behaviour.

S

What can you do if they seem upset?

Our old favourites rule OK here, just as they do in most other similar circumstances: communication, understanding, and reassurance. Talk to your siblings; be open about how you feel towards them (how long is it since you told your sister or brother that you love her/him?) and encourage them to be open with you about how they feel. Give them some time. They're important.

Be conscious of old grievances that may bubble up to the surface now. Sit down with your siblings and talk through such grievances, preferably over lunch, dinner, drinks or a coffee so you can compress those grievances into the small boxes they deserve to be in now that you're all grown up.

Be conscious of the hang-ups your siblings may have – e.g. their own marital problems or lack or marital interest, their youth if they're much younger than you, their sadness at losing you as their sole confidant(e). Don't kid yourself or them that everything is going to be exactly the same once you're married, because it isn't.

But it isn't going to be disastrous, either. Convey to your worried sibling that your marriage may shift your priorities around a bit, but at the end of the day you are still siblings and nothing can change that.

And if they still seem distant or resentful?

Use your instincts to know when you're banging your head against a brick wall. If a sibling simply won't respond to your understanding and reassurance, don't go on. After all, you have a wedding to organise. Be consoled by the fact that you have tried to work things out with your sibling and, OK, it hasn't happened for the moment. Give him or her time. The things you have said today may take weeks or months to penetrate through, but with time many things get healed. Angst with an insecure sibling is one of them.

S Speeches

How to devise, plan, write and deliver a wedding speech is a subject that has been very well covered in a selection of other titles from How To Books (including my own *Wedding Speeches for Women*) so I'm not going to duplicate their information here. If you want free advice you may get some from keying **wedding speeches** into Google or another search engine, but having researched the internet fairly thoroughly for *Wedding Speeches For Women* I can tell you that most of the advice you get from websites is relatively lightweight.

What we do need to look at here, though, is the main problems that can arise with wedding speeches, how to anticipate them, and how to deal with them if they occur.

Picking the right speakers

Much as you may want or feel obliged to have the traditional line-up of speakers (bride's father, groom, best man) at your wedding, be realistic. If one or other of them suffers from severe stage fright, or tends to be a bit unreliable especially after a drink or three, think again. As you'll see from Simon's contribution below, some people just aren't the right choice to make a speech.

So use your imagination here. Traditions in most cultures can be relaxed; you don't have to stick to the rules. Remember that this occasion is not a business or political conference where specific speeches have to be given by specific speakers, or else. As long as the speakers at your wedding remember amongst them who to toast and who to thank, they can be pretty well anyone. That means you should choose the people who a) want to do it, and b) are capable of carrying it off successfully – not people you feel obliged to ask even though you suspect they will either freeze in terror or drone on in a monotone for 45 minutes.

Lost for words

What happened was that the groom suffered from becoming 'hysterically mute'. What that actually means is that he couldn't speak through fear! He stood, he opened his mouth, he spoke ... and silence followed.

The problem, of course, was that he became more and more upset at this, making the situation worse. It's one of the few examples of true 'stage fright' that I've seen. At first the guests were confused, then restless.

The best man proved he was the best man. He simply stepped in and took over. It was a work of genius, because he defused the situation with a joke then started to work the script, changing it as he went to make it sound like it was 'his': gradually he included the groom by asking questions which needed yes/no answers, then more open questions, then, eventually saying 'I'm making a hash of this story: you'd better finish it if you want to prove you weren't as drunk as I'm claiming you were!'

The groom duly finished the story and carried on. At the end, when the toast was proposed, you couldn't hear the words for the cheers and whistles. In a bizarre way it really made the event.

Dr Simon Raybould
Curved Vision, UK
www.curved-vision.co.uk

S

Preparation

In the hustle and bustle of wedding preparations it's all too easy to leave preparation of the wedding speeches until everything else has been done. And that's what often happens; a few thoughts get scribbled in eyebrow pencil on the back of an envelope the night before the wedding.

Some speakers can get away with preparation as sketchy as that, but there aren't many of them. The rest regret it the next day when they realise they haven't thought through what they're going to say and find themselves stumbling around in an embarrassing fashion.

I know I have an axe to grind here (I write a lot of speeches for other people as well as for myself), but please, don't underestimate the importance of doing some preparation for your speech and ensuring that the other speakers involved do likewise.

Sensitive issues

In *Wedding Speeches for Women* I strongly recommend that all speakers due to perform at a wedding get together at least via telephone or email to decide on who is going to cover what topics, and also so that someone can brief everyone on any topics that should be avoided in case they give offence. All speech-givers should research what they're going to talk about, so they know beforehand of any potential banana skins.

As Susan says in her contribution below, 'If you are giving a speech at a wedding, make sure you do some in-depth research ahead of time!' That's the best way to prevent someone saying something in a speech that upsets the bride, groom, a parent, child or other important participant.

Do your homework

I am a public speaking and presentation skills coach based in Dubai, United Arab Emirates, a nation that is a melting pot of cultures (although I guess that could be said of everywhere these days!).

In my workshops people often tell me of public speaking successes and failures. Last year one young man, I believe he was Arab, told me that he had been invited to be the best man at a friend's wedding. I think the couple were Indian. Anyway, in his speech he talked about some of the humorous events that had occurred while the couple had been living together, abroad, over the previous year. Unfortunately, neither the parents of the groom or the bride had been aware that the couple had been co-habiting ... The result, by the young man's account, was a bit of a disaster.

The moral of the story: if you are giving a speech at a wedding, make sure you do some in-depth research ahead of time!

Susan Macaulay, Managing Director
Strike Communications
www.strike.ae / www.amazingwomenonline.com

Humour

I go on at length about the correct use of humour in *Wedding Speeches For Women* and Phil C, Phillip and John – other How To Books authors of wedding speech books – cover the topic very well too. So let me just give you a very short recap not on humour itself, but its potential perils.

The trouble with humour is that it tends to be inwardly focused. In other words what may seem hilarious to you may not even raise a snigger from someone else. If you use humour in a speech – any speech, not just one for a wedding – you need to be sure that the majority of people in the audience will see the joke too. And that becomes particularly important if your wedding guest list includes people from different backgrounds, cultures, religions, ethnic groups, age groups and so on.

There is a way to help ensure this, and that is to use jokes that make fun of circumstances, rather than people. I quote excerpts here from an article of mine that is in wide circulation on the internet:

Use humour about situations, not people. *If you think about it, the butt of many jokes and other humour is a person or group of people, so it's hardly surprising that offence is caused.*

Obviously most humour is going to involve people in one way or another. But as long as the butt of the joke is a situation or set of circumstances, not the people, you're far less likely to upset anyone. And there is an added advantage here.

*Whoever they are and wherever they come from, **people will usually identify with a situation**. Take this one for example ...*

Some people are driving along at night and are stopped by a police car. The officer goes to the driver and warns him that one of the rear lights on his SUV isn't working. The driver jumps out and looks terribly upset. The officer reassures him that he won't get a ticket, it's just a warning, so there's no problem. 'Oh yes there is a problem,' says the man as he rushes towards the back of the car. 'If you could see my rear lights it means I've lost my trailer.'

S

119

As the butt of the joke is the broken rear light and the loss of the trailer, not the policeman or the driver, no one can be offended. And most people can identify with how that would feel.

The other key issue with humour is wordplays, puns, and anything else that's based on figurative speech, slang, or jargon. The short answer is they don't work internationally. However **if the play or double entendre is in the concept rather than the words, it probably will work***.*

These may be funny to us, but would not be understood by anyone who is not a good English speaker because there is a play on the words:

- *Déja moo: the feeling that you've heard this bull before.*

- *The two most common elements in the universe are hydrogen and stupidity.*

These, however, probably would be understood because the humour is in the concept, not in the words themselves:

- *You don't stop laughing because you grow old. You grow old because you stop laughing.*

- *The trouble with doing something right the first time is that nobody appreciates how difficult it was.*

Overcoming nerves

Once again, all of us on the How To Books wedding speech 'team' share some very useful advice on how to overcome stage fright and nerves, so I won't go on about it here.

However, there is one issue that I go on about at length in *Wedding Speeches For Women* and I won't apologise for repeating it here, because it's so important.

If you're giving a speech, don't drink alcohol before you do it. Well, maybe one glass of wine, but even then I would only give that a qualified yes.

As I've banged on about consistently to my speech-giving clients over the last umpty-dump years, do not kid yourself that a glass or two is going to lubricate your vocal chords and engage your brain into issuing witticisms and clever rhetoric. You may think that's what you're putting across after a few snifters, but believe me, it won't be to your guests. You'll just come across as confused and incoherent.

Save the tipples until after the speeches have been given, and try your best to ensure the other speech givers at your wedding are similarly restricted.

Also see sections titled Alcohol, and Nerves and Stress.

Keeping control

If your wedding is to be a fairly large one it may be wise to have someone act as master of ceremonies. Often the services of an MC are offered as part of the package when you book a reception venue. But if not, you can pick an appropriate person from within your family and circle of friends.

What they do is call the guests' attention to the speeches (and possibly the cutting of the cake afterwards). They also can announce the impending arrival of the speeches and politely suggest that anyone needing a comfort break should take one now – particularly important if there are several children in your wedding party.

Also see section titled Comfort Breaks.

Lastly, they can be conscious of rambling speakers and if necessary wind up a long and tedious speech by thanking the speaker profusely for his/her contribution and moving the proceedings on.

Unpleasant surprises

As I have suggested above and elsewhere, a bit of careful planning of the speeches should weed out anyone who, although in theory entitled to speak, may turn out to be a bit of a maverick.

However people are full of surprises and should you find that someone up on his/her feet is performing in a way you feel is inappropriate, this is where the master of ceremonies can cut in and minimise the damage.

What the best man did in Simon's contribution above was brilliant – but you might not be so lucky if the same were to happen to you! However an experienced master of ceremonies (or an amateur well used to public speaking) could get you out of a hole in almost as efficient a fashion.

Forgetting your lines

There's no excuse for this in our enlightened times. While you may not benefit at your wedding from a teleprompt system used by newsreaders and TV presenters, there are such things as cue cards.

If you are giving a speech at a wedding – yours or anyone else's – part of your preparation (see above) should be that you create a set of cards that you can refer to if you need to. Make two sets – keep one in your pack of 'essentials' and give the other to a trusted friend or family member. Be sure to loop the cards together with an elastic band or other device so that if you drop the whole thing, you won't have to grovel around on the floor trying to put the cards in the right order.

And to avoid the need to depend too much on cue cards? Rehearse, rehearse, rehearse.

Shorter is sweeter

Weddings are fun occasions. They are not platforms for lengthy dissertations on the beauties of the bride, the magnanimous generosity of his or her parents, the ins and outs of the groom's activities before he had ever heard of the bride, or any other irrelevancy. (See Steve's contribution below.)

Plan ahead

This was a semi-society wedding ... 200 guests in a small country mansion. The bride's father overdid the 'in praise of my daughter' in his speech and upset some guests. The best man was too rude and pointed and upset more guests, the bride and her parents. The groom seemed to have not prepared at all, thanked his Mum, gave the bridesmaids some flowers, fumbled around and sat down – but it was his family house so perhaps that was ok!

How was it resolved? It wasn't, but some good communication and forward planning would have averted the disaster.

Steve Haley, UK

Bear in mind that wedding guests do not expect a lecture; they expect to share in the joy of the occasion, and share in some light-hearted stuff that everyone can enjoy.

Long speeches at weddings are unpopular, in most cultures. Keep those at your wedding short, tight, to the point and relevant.

More than one language, culture, etc

At my eldest god-daughter's wedding a few years ago the speeches consisted of a real mix of Scottish and French culture (she is Scottish and her husband is French). The vast majority of us 300 or so guests are bilingual, so we really appreciated the fact that the speeches were made to cover both languages.

The father of the groom (French) gave a short speech in French; the father of the bride (Scottish) gave a short speech in English. The groom (a Frenchman) gave a speech in delightfully accented English, and the bride's brother (a Scotsman) gave, as the best man, an equally delightful speech in French.

So sweet ... and so appreciated!

If there is more than one culture/language involved in your wedding, it makes a great deal of sense – not to mention paying respect to the cultures/languages involved – to ensure that the speeches are directed to everyone there. And if that involves a speech or two in different languages, so be it.

Even if it isn't possible to have a whole speech made in one particular language, a few words spoken in that language, especially by the partner whose native tongue it is not, will delight the guests concerned.

Second marriages

In the case of second and subsequent marriages the whole topic of speeches changes completely. Even for traditional-style first marriages the old etiquette is being eroded, but when it comes to second and subsequent weddings you really *can* arrange a speech line up consisting of whoever you want, with no restrictions.

The only proviso I would point out to you is that second marriages are likely to involve a bit more in the way of sensitive issues than would be the case with most first marriages. You may be looking at divorce or widowhood in the recent past, and step-families coming together as a result of this union.

What that may mean is that talking about past events in a speech needs to be handled with extreme care, and possibly is better avoided in favour of talking about the present and the future. This is not the time for anyone to step on others' painful corns.

Also see section titled Second Marriages.

Stag and Hen Nights

And what is this topic doing in a book about wedding worries, one wonders? Could it be that it might have been better to devote the whole book to it?

Stag and hen nights give rise to more pranks and laughs than a barrel full of monkeys could dream up in a millennium. Hence some attendant worries. However, these can be minimised, even if you have friends like those described in Warren's contribution below.

As for stag and hen nights that get out of hand on the night in question, I think it's probably safer for me to say you're on your own. If you get drunk and taken down to a police station to cool off there's little I can do or say that will help, other than advise you to be polite, take some headache pills the next morning, and hope you have wealthy and generous friends who can bail you out.

However there is one thing that, despite getting repeated over and over again by all the wedding books, websites, magazines and other pundits, cannot be emphasised enough. Quite simply, this is: do it some time before the wedding, not the night before. Not even two nights before. The last thing anyone needs on their wedding day is a hangover; and remember, bad ones can last for two days or more.

An excuse for a good time?

I'm not sure how the history of stag (and later hen) nights evolved, but in our enlightened times it's hardly necessary for the bride and groom to go out for an evening separately in order to celebrate their 'last day of free-dom'. Most couples nowadays socialise separately as well as together so to postulate that the stag or hen night is essential in the light of an impending marriage is, frankly, BS.

What the stag or hen night does, though, is provide both bride and groom with a handy opportunity to disappear for a few hours, or even days, with their friends and forget temporarily about wedding plans, stress, frustrations and obligations. Even if that does result in excess consumption of alcohol and some serious hangovers, it's still healthy for its stress-relieving properties.

You don't necessarily have to go out and get plastered

Here's a surprise; the stag or hen do does not necessarily have to involve riotous behaviour and endless boozing to fulfil its objectives as a welcome diversion from wedding plans fairly close to the day itself.

The guys don't have to get blind drunk at the pub, eat a fierce curry and then watch some sleazy striptease. Instead they can have a session at the gym, a game of golf, or even a weekend away golfing or watching their favourite football team play somewhere in Europe.

The girls don't have to hit the cocktail bars or clubs; they can book into a health spa to be pampered and massaged for a day or a weekend, or even jet off to a romantic European capital city for a weekend of culture, good company and reasonable quantities of local wine.

Watch out for unscrupulous profiteers

There has been a story in the news at the time I'm writing this (late 2006) about scams in eastern European cities popular for stag weekends. The men, already somewhat overly refreshed, are lured into nightclubs and then mugged for their money, passports and other valuables. Be warned.

Even in the UK less-than-honest restaurant and club owners can see a pre-wedding stag or hen do coming, and will rub their hands together in glee at the prospect of over-charging the entire party. It's best if someone can pre-negotiate a deal with the restaurant or club if a pre-booking is possible, so there is a lower risk of unpleasant surprises on the night.

What if budgets are restricted?

Here, think the great outdoors and nature, because to a large extent it's free.

How about a camping trip to a beauty spot somewhere in your region?

How about an outing to a beautiful stately home, followed by lunch in the local pub?

How about a trip to a nearby theme park? (They don't just cater for children – and doing all the rides with a group of adult friends can be terrific fun.)

How about a night out to greyhound racing (the dogs)? Or a day out to a local point-to-point horse race, assuming it's the right season?

How about a picnic on a beach, or in some other local beauty spot? The picnic can, of course, contain alcohol for the non-drivers.

Use your imagination, and your knowledge of what you and your friends can really get into. With a little creative thinking there are many things you can do for a stag or hen night that will cost little, but mean a lot.

What really matters

My overall message? Don't feel obliged to spend fortunes on getting wasted just because you feel that's what's expected of you. Think about what you really want to do, and encourage your fiancé to do the same, without anyone being influenced by friends, family, tradition or anything else. Remember whose wedding it is, and what will make you happy.

And last of all, enjoy!

Legging it

On a stag do near RAF Wroughton (Military Hospital) one of the staff had invited all of the blokes from work. They got him so blind drunk he passed out, fell over and broke his leg. Needless to say the next day he woke up with his leg in plaster, a wife-to-be furious that in three weeks' time the wedding photos would have him in a leg cast.

According to the X-rays his leg was broken in two places – what luck he was out with hospital staff who despite being p*ssed themselves knew how to react.

On the morning of the wedding, just as they were about to cut the suit trousers so he could get in them, they cut off his cast instead and confessed they just couldn't resist when he passed out. No broken leg, and three weeks on crutches, putting up with ear ache from the missus. Brilliant!!

Warren Cass, UK
www.business-scene.com

Stationery

See sections titled Guests, and Second Marriages.

Superstitions

A load of rubbish... or should you take them seriously?

Much as we may be modern thinkers and dismiss any kind of hocus-pocus as, well, hocus-pocus, most brides do pay a little sneaky regard to superstitions and how they may affect the outcome of the wedding and the marriage.

Being a pragmatic type I have to say that superstitions should not be taken seriously. But then, why do I refuse to walk under a ladder, or feel overjoyed when I find a four-leafed clover?

Let's take a look at some of the more commonly known wedding superstitions – just for the sake of academic interest, of course!

Bows

It seems you should gather together all the bows and ribbons from the wrapping of your wedding gifts, stick them together into a large bouquet, and hang them over your marital front door for about a year. This apparently brings good luck. It will also bring cobwebs, dust and all manner of other creepy crawlies to your new home. Perhaps pressing all the bows into a flat collage, duly framed with insect-proof glass, would be more appropriate?

Chimney sweep

Many sources say it's good luck if the bride sees, or preferably is kissed by, a chimney sweep on her wedding day. Just be sure you're not wearing your pristine white dress at the time.

Green

For some reason I can't fathom the colour green is considered unlucky not only for weddings, but for cars and many other things. Being a typical Taurean who loves the countryside and anything naturally green I must protest, but equally I owe it to you to convey the superstition, so there you go. (Mind you, would anyone wear green at their wedding?)

Knives as gifts

Jewish traditions say that if you receive knives as gifts (and oh, wouldn't I love to receive a set of decent kitchen knives!) it's bad luck (oh, no, it wouldn't be in my case). Anyway the remedy is for the recipient to give the donor a coin, so demoting the gift to a business transaction which solves the problem.

Rain on wedding day

This is an interesting one. Many superstitions say it's bad luck if it rains on your wedding day, others say it's good luck. Maybe that depends on which hemisphere you live in, or at least which climate. Those of us who live in chronically rainy Northern Europe should probably assume that rain on our wedding day is just one of those blasted things that we have to deal with whatever event we're organising. However if you're of a romantic frame of mind ... rain on your wedding day can mean fertility via good news for the farmers' crops. Some cultures say rain on your wedding day means you will have many children.

Finally, if you're a Roman Catholic, I'm told that hanging a rosary outside on your clothes line if it's raining on your wedding morning will ensure the downpour stops in time for the big event. I wish it were that easy...

Rice, throwing after ceremony

This tradition goes back quite a long way and the little rice kernels are supposed to represent fertility despite their being a squillion times larger than reproductive ova. (Confetti and flower petals represent the same thing.) Rice is also a damned nuisance in the yards of wedding ceremony venues because the kernels tend to acquire dampness, swell up and get caught up in the soles of everyone's shoes – especially trainers. Before you allow rice to be thrown, check it out with the powers-that-be at your ceremony to ensure it's permitted.

Right foot forward

This one is a bit like the old children's superstition, 'Step on a crack, break your grandmother's back.' It seems the bride must step into the wedding ceremony venue with her right foot first for good luck. Just watch you don't catch it in the hem of your dress.

Something old, something new, something borrowed, something blue

(And a silver sixpence in her shoe.) It seems this rhyme first emerged in Victorian times, but its origins go back further. The meaning of each item is not clear, but generally it's taken that something old refers to the background of the couple – their friends and family. This is symbolised by the bride wearing something that isn't new. Something new is about the couple's future together, and shouldn't be hard to symbolise as chances are the bride's entire outfit is new – or at least new to her which is all that matters.

Something borrowed should be something belonging to a happily married family member so their good fortune carries on to the bride, and some say you should be sure to return the item if you want to avoid bad luck. Yes, even if you borrow your grandmother's diamond earrings.

Something blue seems to have a variety of origins including ancient Rome, early Christianity and the Jewish faith. Take your pick.

Finally, the sixpence in your shoe. You would be hard pushed to find a sixpence these days since it was taken out of circulation in 1980. However if you insist on this one you can obtain a silver sixpence (they weren't always made of silver) from this website: www.silver6pence.com.

Spider in the wedding gown

Many sources say that if you find a spider in your wedding gown, that's a symbol of good luck. Probably not if you're arachnophobic, however.

Tears
Oh, dear, this is a confusing one. There are many different and conflicting superstitions about the relevance of the bride crying at her wedding. The majority say it means that you'll never cry again in your marriage, which is good news, but if you do your mascara will run, which isn't. Decisions, decisions.

Throwing the bride's bouquet.
Tradition says the bride should call all interested female parties to gather around her, turn her back on them, and throw her bouquet over her shoulder. Whoever catches it is next to be married. Either that or the lucky lady will get a jaunty black eye from catching a heavy bunch of blooms in her face.

Throwing the bride's garter
A similar tradition says that the groom should remove his new wife's garter and, having gathered all his single male friends around him, he should then throw that over his shoulder. Whoever catches it is the next man to be married. Mind you if the bride still has her dress hitched up from having had the garter removed, the men's attention may well be elsewhere.

Tin cans
This is my favourite. According to one perfectly serious source, the act of tying tin cans to the back bumper of the wedding car ensures that evil spirits will be warded off. Riding in a car would suggest 21st century timing to me; aren't we a bit too modern to believe in evil spirits? I must have missed something.

Veils
Originally veils were worn to hide the bride away from evil spirits (and bridesmaids all dressed alike were suppose to confuse, thereby inhibit, evil spirits). In later cultures veils were worn more as a mark of chastity and modesty. And besides, they look lovely.

Wearing white
Some say that wearing the colour white for your wedding has diddly squat to do with the old virginity myth, but is purely a matter of financial one-upmanship. Evidently in the old days it was very costly to bleach fabrics and the whiter a fabric was, the more it must have cost the people concerned – hence the desirability of a whiter-than-white fabric for the wedding dress. Having seen numerous friends married in white when they were several months pregnant, I don't think the virginity gag stands up any more. But hey – if you want to wear white, why not.

Wedding dress, making your own

Many people believe it's unlucky for the bride to make her own wedding dress. I would agree entirely. Most brides are so busy trying to organise the wedding, do their jobs, and have a life, that to take on the huge project of making your own wedding dress as well would be bound to make you very unlucky. That's purely because the extra work and stress would land you in the funny farm months before the wedding.

Wedding vows, when you say them

A common superstition is that you should be married and say your vows when the hour hand on the clock is on its way up, rather than on its way down. I don't know where that superstition comes from, but suspect it may be connected with pub opening times in the UK and the fact that grooms in the old days didn't want to miss their drinking opportunities.

S

Ushers

See section titled Best Man and Ushers.

Venues

Choosing a venue is probably the most important element of planning your wedding, other than – perhaps – getting engaged! I talk about religious venues in the section titled Churches, Synagogues and other Religious Venues, and reception venues below. Also see sections titled Caterers; Confetti; Decorations; Directions and Parking; Entertainment; Flowers; Guests; Marquees; Outdoor Weddings; Civil Partnerships; Civil Weddings; Seating Plans and Wedding Planners.

Picking the right venue for your reception depends on a number of issues including budget, number of guests, personal preference, etc. Other wedding books and websites cover this topic in some detail, but here are some of the more common problems you can run into, and what you can do to avoid them.

1. The venue is not conveniently located for guests to access

Romantic though a small hotel on a remote Scottish island may be, if most of your friends and family live in the south-east of England it will be difficult and expensive for them to get there and many will refuse the invitation because of that. You need to weigh up how important their presence is, against the romantic desirability of the location. Think carefully and be sure you make the right decision for you.

2. The venue is not well equipped for wedding receptions

Equally, a romantic castle in Ireland may be a beautiful setting, but if it has poor heating, antiquated or non-existent kitchens and is miles away from the nearest large town, it's going to cost a lot of money to bring all the necessary facilities in. The other problem here is that you, or someone else, will have to spend a lot of time and effort on organising the whole thing and if it is a long way from where you/the other person live, it could be a logistical nightmare. Fear not … there *are* romantic venues in Ireland that do have all you need!

3. The venue is very popular for weddings

You may have to book this some months if not a year or more in advance, and even then if your wedding is during the 'wedding season' – especially towards the end of the season – you may find the venue looks a bit tired, staff are a bit tired, facilities are over-worked, and bits of yesterday's reception are still lurking deep in the carpets. A good, but slightly less popular venue might be the better choice, as they will probably be trying harder right to the end of the season.

4. The venue is what you've always wanted, but is more than you can afford

Who says you have to do a full sit down meal, or even a buffet meal? Who says you have to have an afternoon/evening reception? And who says you have to pick a Saturday or Sunday (unless there are religious reasons) instead of a non-peak day and time? Many venues are only too glad to do good deals for receptions held outside the traditional circumstances because they take up downtime which would otherwise be unprofitable. See sections listed above, and also especially Finances and Budgeting, and Food and Drink.

5. The venue of your dreams is abroad

See section titled Destination Weddings.

V

Videography

Here's where I hand over to yet another expert!

Although I have worked with corporate and documentary TV (as a scriptwriter) for more years than I care to admit to, wedding videos are something I know little about and so have handed over here to someone who really is an expert: Peter Snell of Clicks Media Studios – winner of such UK titles as Professional Videographer of the Year, and that of UK Top Wedding Video Producer.

Advice from UK professional videographer, Peter Snell

Nothing can bring the emotions of a wedding back to life in quite the same way as a well-crafted video. It should make you laugh and cry at exactly the right moments, and is something to be treasured for a lifetime.

A wedding is about the most challenging event to film as it is 80% spontaneous and you only get one 'take'.

Part of the problem is that it is quite common for people starting out in the video business to begin by making wedding videos because they mistakenly see them as an easy way to get started. To make matters worse, once they become competent they often abandon weddings to do commercial work. The result is that in some areas wedding videography is disproportionately serviced by inexperienced people.

However this just means you need to be careful as there are plenty of excellent videographers who actually love doing weddings. The key is to find out about their experience.

Occasionally things can go wrong and, like most horror stories, they are usually based on a lack of knowledge and a breakdown in communication, as the bride is expecting Hollywood blockbuster results on an Indie budget.

There are many things to look for when hiring a wedding videographer, but the critical factor is experience.

Wedding videos are a specialist product and you need someone who understands the genre inside and out.

Look for a member, preferably qualified, of a trade association such as IOV (Institute of Videography www.iov.co.uk).

Ask to see a demo of the videographer's previous work. If they say they can't supply a demo for privacy or other reasons, cross them off your list. Ideally you should see a range of work from them, and also make sure you watch an entire video from start to finish. You want to know that they can cover the whole event well, not just get a few nice shots here and there.

You might also like to ask for references from previous customers.

The videographer should be able to get on with people and communicate well. Effective communication is important to make the day run smoothly, as well as making sure that everyone knows what to do and what to expect in relation to the video.

Videographers need to work with both guests and other professionals. If possible get the celebrant, photographer and videographer, etc to meet at the rehearsal to discuss each other's needs.

Different videographers have different styles and you should choose one that you are comfortable with. What style the videographer does best will be revealed when you see examples of his/her work. Common styles include:

- fly-on-the-wall, reality-TV style

- documentary, including interviews, voice-overs, etc

- arty, cinematic styles.

We can't give a specific price guide here because they vary so much from place to place, but professional videography is usually at least as expensive as professional photography. Remembering that most videos require several days of skilled labour with expensive equipment, you can see why good video production costs a lot.

It is definitely worth asking how many cameras will be used. A single camera in the hands of an experienced videographer can capture all aspects of the day and produce a very entertaining film.

Two manned cameras will allow for a greater variety of shots, especially during the service. A third camera, usually left on a static wide shot, can provide additional safety and creative options.

Good quality editing is very important and will make a massive difference. Ask these questions:

- **How long will the final product be?**

Long videos are usually offered by the inexperienced videographer. They contain everything, including the umms and errs, and are likely to have the feel of a home movie as they have less editing. The experienced videographer is more likely to produce everything you expect to see and hear, but in a shorter TV style film.

- **Can you have more than one version, e.g. a longer version for family, a highlights version for showing friends and a warts and all version (raw footage) for personal nostalgia?**

If you are concerned about budget, one option is to ask for the wedding to be recorded but not edited. The 'raw' footage, which isn't practical to watch, can be saved and edited later when you can afford it. The most important thing is to capture the day — editing can wait if necessary.

V

The most important things you need to do to help the videographer do a good job:

- Nominate a reliable person to liaise with the videographer throughout the day.

- Provide maps, telephone numbers and contact names for venues and key people.

- Provide details of key guests and order of service so that the camera is in the right place at the right time and Aunty Glad in British Columbia gets sent best wishes!

- Reserve a parking place as close as possible to the venue. The videographer needs to move quickly and the equipment can be heavy.

- Liaise with the celebrant so the videographer has a good, clear view of the couple's faces as they take their vows, unobstructed by alter screens, choirs, flower arrangements.

- Advise guests that an official videographer will be present and will appreciate their co-operation. If they want to be camera-shy it is up to them to make themselves scarce rather than make themselves look ridiculous by running away or making silly faces and comments.

Using an amateur videographer

If you must use an amateur videographer, here are the most important things he or she should bear in mind.

- Check out their past work. When on holiday did they tell a story? Did the camera follow the action or was it out of focus with zooms, pans and camera shake that made you feel seasick?

- When people were speaking, could they be heard clearly or did the background and wind noise over-power the voices?

- Never buy a camera and give it to your nephew the day before – the operator and the camera need to work as one. Give them time to read the camera's manual thoroughly.

- Make sure they know how to focus and change the 'white balance'.

- Relying on automatic settings usually results in bad colour balance, out of focus shots, loss of definition and blown-out pictures, producing dark silhouettes instead of smiles and tears. Just setting a camera for indoor or outdoor use can make a lot of difference to the quality of footage.

- A tripod is essential for stable shots. No one can hold a camera still for long periods of time (during service and speeches) without wobble, especially if they are using the zoom because they are outside the action zone. The tripod should be smooth and sturdy.

- Always have more than enough tapes, batteries, cables, chargers, etc – back-up equipment in general. Never rely on mains power being available where you want it or expecting batteries to last all day, or expect to get everything you want on one tape. Recommend that they change tapes after service/wedding breakfast/evening dance as changing tapes in the middle of the action can be disastrous.

- Never rely only on the camera microphone – a better mike can make a lot of difference.

- Ensure there is a muffler on all microphones. Wind noise (*or speakers' 'pops and bangs'*) can easily drown out voices or compromise the soundtrack.

- Additional microphones are needed if the vows and speeches are to be recorded clearly.

- When editing, remember that you don't have to use everything you filmed – less is more.

- Try to limit the use of filters and fancy transitions (exploding pages, wipes, turning page effects, etc).

- Keep the edited footage flowing and interesting.

- Before using commercial music ensure that the appropriate licences have been purchased (MCPS and PPL).

Peter Snell
Clicks Media Studios
01634 723838
info@clicksstudios.co.uk

Where Peter mentions trade associations to which your videographer might well belong, it's worth also crediting members of the APV – the Association of Professional Videomakers, www.apv.org.uk.

V

Wedding Insurance

Many companies offer wedding insurance and this can be a very good idea, especially with the unpredictable lives we seem to lead.

For a relatively modest premium these policies will cover the cost of problems arising from wedding dresses, wedding clothes hire, transport, gifts, photographer and photographs, the wedding video, the rings, deposits lost due to bankruptcy of suppliers, wedding cakes, public liability, etc.

As with any insurance purchase, shop around and read the small print. And be warned; most wedding insurance does not cover you for cancellation due to the bride and groom splitting up!

Also see section titled Postponement or Cancellation.

For more information key **wedding insurance** into Google or another search engine, or look it up in the Wedding Guide of your local *Yellow Pages*.

Wedding Lists

See section titled Gifts and Gift Lists.

Wedding Planners

Wedding planners are very popular in the USA and are becoming more popular here in the UK.

They do cost money, but most claim to be able to save you money on wedding costs due to their professional buying power. If you and your fiancé are very busy people, what you spend on a wedding planner may be well worth it for taking the burden of all the organisation off your shoulders.

Wedding planners can also be very helpful in families where there is likely to be a bit of dictatorial behaviour on the part of a parent or other close relative. It may be relatively easy to get bossy with a son or a daughter, but it's a lot harder with a cool, professional stranger who knows more about weddings than you do.

To find wedding planners, key **wedding planners** into Google or another search engine, or look up the Wedding Guide in your local *Yellow Pages*.

I asked Bernadette, Britt and Kelly from the UK Alliance of Wedding Planners to tell us just what a wedding planner can do, and advise us on how to work with one.

Advice from professional wedding planners

Many wedding planners offer a range of services to suit most budgets and weddings. As a guide, full planning will cost between 10%–15% of the bride's budget. Co-ordinating just the wedding day tends to range from £250-£700. During the initial phone call the wedding planner will ask the bride questions to ascertain exactly what services she wants or needs to assist her with her wedding. So, at the top, it could be the full planning service which would include finding the venue, booking all suppliers, deciding on a theme and managing the day itself. At the bottom, it can be just one or a selection of the above services.

Value for money

Most reputable planners negotiate discounts from their suppliers which are then passed on to the bride. These discounts are only given to wedding planners who offer the supplier repeat business which one hopes the bride won't do. Also, a wedding planner ensures the bride's money is spent effectively and not wasted on suppliers or items not needed or that are overpriced. Plus, she will ensure all suppliers offer competitive rates.

Working alongside

A bride and groom should never feel left out by the wedding planner. It is their wedding and the wedding planner has been hired to ensure they get the wedding they want. Wedding planners provide all the options to the couple whether it is design, suppliers or venue choices, from which the couple make the final decision. The wedding planner should be working alongside the couple, doing the legwork, coming up with creative ideas to enhance the bridal couple's ideas and making sure that everything is going smoothly.

Family politics is the norm when you are a wedding planner. The key is to listen to all sides of the story and give the correct etiquette answer, but also a modern alternative. A good planner does not automatically take the bride's side, but tries to view the whole picture objectively, acting in an assertive manner and aims to provide solutions to suit everyone. Oh and, actually, Mums tend to love us!

Weddings are very complex now with the average spend £20,000. Couples are working longer hours leaving little time to actually organise their wedding. On top of that, people are tending to move away from home to establish themselves, whether it is abroad or a different part of their home country. As a result, when it comes to their wedding, they may look to marry in their home town, but are reluctant to leave all the planning to their parents. This is where an independent professional comes in, recommending local suppliers and working closely with the couple. There are also many couples who live abroad, come home to marry and feel they need the extra support of someone 'on the ground'. On a separate note, as couples are older as they get married, they may have been to several corporate events which have led them to appreciate the professional touches on events and they wish to have that same polish applied to their wedding.

DIY wedding planning

Ask for help from family and friends. Delegate tasks to those you trust implicitly and are known for their organisational skills. You would be surprised how many relatives have hidden talents like cake making, flower arranging, etc. Ask around for someone who has a nice car to use rather then hiring a wedding car. Then once everything is in place, hire a wedding planner to take over in the final few weeks and co-ordinate on the day itself.

Bernadette Chapman, Britt Armstrong Gash and Kelly Chandler
UK Alliance of Wedding Planners Ltd
www.akawp.com

Wedding Websites and Weblogs

What would we do without the internet? This extraordinary communication tool has become so much a part of most people's lives that to find yourself suddenly bereft of an online connection seems more inconvenient than having one leg cut off.

Thanks to this technology we are now able to enjoy instant communication with people anywhere in the world – not just via the text of emails, but also via video and audio links. This means that if you want (and can afford it) your wedding ceremony in the UK can be shown live to your great-grandmother in New Zealand.

Are they worth it?

You'll find some very positive thoughts on this question in Namrata's contribution below. And although she has a vested interest in promoting the idea, actually it is a good one.

You don't necessarily have to go the lengths of hiring a website service, although as Namrata points out to organise and update a website yourself does involve time that may be in short supply. However, creating and updating your wedding site is a job that could be delegated to a bright teenage relative or friend. There are numerous packages and services available that will provide you with the software you need, a domain name (e.g. www.brianandkatiewedding.org) and everything else you need for a reasonable cost. To find these, key **make your own website** into Google or another search engine.

You can use the website to update all your friends and relatives about your wedding plans, and you can exchange messages with everyone you need to even if they are on the other side of the world. The site can also supply details of accommodation locally, flight, train, or coach schedules, your wedding list, directions on how to get to the wedding ceremony and reception, plus all other information that's relevant. There's more it can achieve, too – see Namrata's contribution below.

W

Advice from a wedding website service provider

A wedding website saves time, energy and money for the couple. All three are at a premium when you are getting married. An extra hour of sleep can get back the glow on your face and you could use the additional balance in your card to experience the luxurious spa during your honeymoon.

- A wedding website makes your special day even more memorable. It allows you to announce your wedding plans and share your precious memories and photos with all your guests, in an elegant and personal way.

- Wedding websites allow you, as a couple, to share all the details of your wedding with friends and family no matter where they live.

- A wedding website will save you time, energy and money. Just include your website address on your wedding invite and no more dealing with endless phone calls and emails. You can answer all queries with, 'It's on the website'.

- A wedding website will enhance your guests' experience, allowing them to view your wedding plans, and if you so wish, make suggestions and have a role in planning your wedding.

- Passing your wedding albums around to show your family and friends, or inviting people home to see your photos can be time-consuming. It can be even more difficult when your nearest and dearest are spread across different parts of the world! A wedding website puts it all in one place for everyone to see. Simply upload some photos online and let them enjoy them sooner rather than later.

- You can also update your website with honeymoon photos and comments; everyone will love to hear about your trip.

- You know friends are also waiting for you to bring your wedding CD over, so why make them wait? Webcast your wedding ceremonies so that even those who missed the big day can get a feel of what it was like.

Cost

If you compare it with the time and cost of making a thousand phone calls a wedding website definitely comes cheaper. Think of that 20-minute conversation with your aunt in Sydney. And she wanted to know more! But with a wedding website, you can answer all questions with this: 'It is there on our website!'

How it works

If you use a wedding website 'service' provider, it is effortless and takes no time. All you need to do is FedEx a copy of the wedding photos and video and email the text. We completely take it up from there and by the time you have unpacked your honeymoon bags your wedding story is up on the internet.

In the case of you signing up for a 'template based' wedding website, then the time taken for updating would depend on the ease of the web interface and 'how much you want to tell'. It could take anything from a couple of hours to a few days.

I know it is cheaper to email friends, but easier, no! And how many emails? What if you miss out a few people? Your wedding website is a single point of information on everything related to your wedding. It announces your wedding, introduces your fiancé to your friends, gives info on the wedding venue, date, time, tells them about how you met, shows your wedding pictures and video. It does all that you would need to do a hundred times over.

Through a wedding website, all the important details are easily available to your guests in one place. You even put up a Google Map (or similar reference) of the wedding venue and sit back and enjoy the foot massage.

How long a wedding website lasts depends on the wedding package you purchased from the vendor. It could be from a month to a year or beyond.

A wedding website should ideally stay for at least six to eight months after the wedding. This would give ample time to the people who could not attend your wedding to get a virtual experience of it and know who got the bride's garter. Those who were a part of the wedding will also be able to see themselves (and who was that babe in red?) in the wedding pictures and order a copy if required.

Namrata Manot
MyDreamShaadi
www.mydreamshaadi.in

What about a wedding weblog?

Using a weblog or 'blog' to chronicle and update people on your wedding plans is a simple and cheap alternative to a website, and can even incorporate pictures and other bits and pieces. You can set up a weblog for free through one of many services available. To find one, key **create a blog** into Google or other search engine.

Who Pays What?

See section titled Finances and Budgeting.

Zero Hour... Disaster Recovery Tips!

Breath not too fresh

What with stress, excitement, little food, some alcohol and various other challenges, your breath may not be as fresh as you'd like it to be all day long. Pack some breath freshener or sweets and keep them handy. They'll also help if you find your mouth and throat getting a bit dry.

Car won't start

Make sure you have a standby – anything will do – that you know is reliable and will 'get you to the church on time', as the line goes in the old musical *My Fair Lady*. No matter how much other people may assure you that the vehicle in question is foolproof, be a cynic and demand that the standby should be available even so. This is one time when you do not want your cynicism to be proven right.

Caterers don't turn up

This is an extremely unlikely possibility, but it has been known. Know where the best local restaurants and takeaways are located. If all else fails despatch someone to go and fetch extra drinks and snacks from the nearest pub or supermarket. Then in the meantime call or send another volunteer to the local food outlets to see what they can do in a short space of time and then, relax. Fish and chips with champagne? Why not?

Disco/entertainment doesn't turn up

Once again this is an unlikely possibility, but you can allow for it in your plans. Make sure you have a stock of recorded music in a form that's compatible with the playback system at your venue. Ensure that these items are readily available at your reception. With luck you won't need any of it, but should push come to shove you will be prepared.

Dress gets stained

Many shops sell stain-removal wipes and kits; invest in the best available pack and make sure it's available at all times throughout the ceremony and reception. A good place to keep it is in the handbag of someone who is likely to be near you most of the time – mother, mother-in-law, sister.

Dress gets torn

This may seem obvious, but make sure someone in the bridal party has a needle and some cotton/thread available. Failing that, there are some adhesive substances available which will stick fabric together at very short notice. Your local haberdashery counter in a department store will have some ideas; alternatively, your local ironmongers or supermarket will have appropriate products. Buy some before the big day and have it handy. And if even that fails? Use some double-sided sticky tape. It may not be a solution that lasts for months, but right now all that counts is a few hours – and here that should do the trick.

Flowers make you sneeze

Well, if flowers make you sneeze it would seem you have some sort of allergy and therefore should be having treatment for it already. However if, like me, you're just an occasional hay fever sufferer, do yourself a favour and buy some over-the-counter antihistamine tablets which you can pop should your floral choice make you sniffy.

Forget speech

I deal with how to avoid this problem at some length in the section titled Speeches, but should you get the Big Freeze at the last moment, don't panic. Remember why you're there and what your role is. It's not rocket science, and you are not expected to deliver a Dimbleby lecture. All you need to do, really, is toast the people you've been assigned to toast, say a few nice things about the bridal party and then sit down and relax. Don't forget that. If all else fails and you forget or freeze up what you have prepared, just say the basics, smile, and sit down. That's all that really matters.

Hair goes wrong

Ach, this is a tough one. So many wedding hairstyles are incredibly elaborate and should the construction of that elaborate style go wrong, you might think that the end of the world has come. Don't. Please do not forget that your natural beauty is going to shine through on this day more that any other. If your elaborate hairstyle doesn't work say nuts to it all, brush it all through, place your tiara/head-dress on again (if you want to) and go for it. Your inner beauty will more than outshine any hair hiccups you could imagine.

Headaches

The stress and hyperactivity of a wedding day can give many people headaches, so pack some paracetamol or ibuprofen in someone handy's pocket or bag. If there's room somewhere readily available, a small bottle of mineral or spring water is a useful idea too.

Heel breaks off your shoe

Put a pack of super glue in with your makeup emergency kit (see below.) Preferably get someone else to do the sticking together, in case you get some superglue on your fingers!

Hired clothes wrong size

Most people involved in the wedding advisory business emphasise how important it is to ensure that whatever clothes are hired for a wedding are not only sized appropriately at the ordering stage, but also are tried on and confirmed at least a few days before the wedding so should there be an embarrassing mistake, there's time to get something done about it. Strictly speaking this is more likely to be an issue for the boys to consider. But don't ignore it. Please.

Important person gets drunk

In all honesty, when you're making plans for a wedding you're very likely to know who amongst the key people is likely to get drunk and probably, at what stage of the proceedings. If you want to play it utterly safe, don't place all your hopes for a decent performance on such a person. Allow them the benefit of the doubt by all means, but don't stress yourself out wondering whether person X will manage to get there sober. Have an alternative on standby who can take over – or better still, pick a more reliable type in the first place.

Lose rings

Once again this is an extremely unlikely option, but it *can* happen. Should that be the case, get your bridal attendants to ask around quickly if someone is willing to lend their ring/rings. Obviously those can be returned as soon as the offending items are found again, but borrowed items can be seen as OK by most religions – in an emergency. What matters at the end of the day is not the symbols, like rings, but the actuality of your marriage. No sweat.

Makeup emergency kit

Remember this will have to be lodged in a safe place like the handbag of a close relative, so everything must be small-sized. However try if you can to include spare lipsticks, compressed powder (appropriate colours for bride and bridesmaids,) tissues, a small mirror, comb, brush, small container of hairspray, etc).

Makeup smears

Have a small pack of makeup remover pads included in your makeup emergency kit (see above.) Remove the smear with the pad, cover over with concealer the same colour as your foundation then apply compressed powder, eyeshadow, lipstick, blusher, etc as appropriate.

Mobile phones

You'd think everyone would be aware of this one by now, but believe me people still forget to switch their phones off or to silent during weddings and other ceremonial occasions, only to be frazzled with embarrassment when the things go off at exactly the wrong moment. However don't be tempted to leave yours at home, because if something should go wrong at the last minute you'll have it handy. Just remember to switch it off.

Z

Nail breaks

Pack a pair of nail scissors and an emery board in your makeup emergency kit (see above) plus a bottle of the varnish you have used to do your nails, so you can touch up. Depending on how the nail has broken you may be able to stick it back together with the superglue (see above).

Nerves get to you

I've gone into some detail about this earlier in the book under Nerves and Stress. However sometimes an attack of nerves can catch you unawares. Should that happen stop yourself for a moment and breathe in and out slowly and gently. Sit down if you can, especially if you feel faint. Concentrate on your breathing and feel how it helps you relax. Continue breathing gently, slowly, but fully as you get up and start off again. Many people swear by Bach Rescue Remedy, a herbal preparation, as an instant help to get you through a traumatic moment or two. You may find it helpful to include some of this stuff in your makeup emergency kit; it's available in a variety of forms from most pharmacies in the UK.

Photographer doesn't turn up

At most weddings there will be several people among the guests who will bring their cameras. If your photographer doesn't turn up pick one or two people who know how to use their cameras and ask them to take some pictures of the early stages of your wedding, at least. Provided that they're using digital cameras you will be able to see whether the shots are any good right away, and reshoot any that don't turn out too well. This way if the photographer does eventually turn up, you won't necessarily have to stage the early photo setups again for his or her benefit.

Power failure at reception

Most dedicated function venues have a backup generator system in place so even if there is a powercut they can still provide electricity. If your venue is in a less usual place, or at home, you won't have this benefit. To allow for powercuts when there is no reason to suspect one is likely may be a little too pessimistic! However if your venue is in an area known to be prone to powercuts, or if thunderstorms are predicted on the day, it's a good idea to have at least some of the menu consisting of cold dishes and to prepare a supply of candles or gas lights.

Tights/pantyhose/stocking ladder/run

Include in your makeup emergency kit a bottle of clear nail varnish, and dab some of this on each end of the ladder. That will stop it progressing any further. It's also a good idea for the bride to have a spare pair of tights or stockings available, especially if you're going to make an issue of removing the garter.

Time of the month approaching

If your wedding day is anywhere near the anticipated date of a period, make sure you put a tampon or two in with the makeup emergency kit (see above.)

Uninvited guests arrive

Here you will need to use your discretion and decide whether to stretch a point and let them in; in some circumstances this is easier than getting into a disagreement. However some uninvited guests are more unwelcome than others. If you think there is any risk at all of such people turning up, warn a few large male family members and friends that their expulsion skills may be required and who they may need to expel. Incidents can usually be kept to a minimum provided everyone is on their toes and deals with any uninvited guests quickly, before things have time to turn into a problem.

Weather is foul

Weather forecasting techniques are getting more accurate every day and even in unpredictable old UK, the Met Office does a pretty good job nowadays of letting us know what weather to expect over a period of at least 24 hours. If you're using a professional bridal car service the chauffeurs will have a stock of umbrellas in the boot ready for a downpour. If you're planning other forms of transport, though, be sure there are sufficient umbrellas available in the vehicle ... and that they all work! If wind is likely to be a problem, the bride and bridesmaids should invest in some large chiffon scarves. These can be tied lightly around hairstyles, tiaras, veils, etc and will keep them in place without squashing them.

Z

Bibliography

How To Books offer a useful selection of self-help books on other wedding topics:

Be the Best, Best Man & Make a Stunning Speech Philip Khan-Panni

The Complete Best Man John Bowden

Make a Great Wedding Speech Philip Calvert

Making a Wedding Speech John Bowden

Making the Best Man's Speech John Bowden

Making the Bridegroom's Speech John Bowden

Making the Father of the Bride's Speech John Bowden

Planning Your Wedding Judith Verity

Wedding Speeches For Women Suzan St Maur

Index